Manchester

Manchester's most popular

Chinese Arts Centre	8	Manchester Museum	20
Cornerhouse	9	Manchester Town Hall	22
Gallery of Costume	10	Manchester United Football Club	24
Hat Works	11	Museum of Science & Industry	26
Imperial War Museum North	12	Ordsall Hall Museum	28
Manchester Airport Aviation		People's History Museum	29
Viewing Park	14	Salford Museum & Art Gallery	30
Manchester Art Gallery	15	The Lowry	32
Manchester Cathedral	16	Urbis	34
Manchester City Football Club	18	Whitworth Art Gallery	35
Manchester Craft & Design Centre	19		

Museums and Heritage Sites · 36-41

Central Manchester	36-38	Greater Manchester	38-41

Art Galleries and Exhibitions · 42-47

Central Manchester	42-45	Greater Manchester	45-47

Music, Theatre and the Performing Arts · 48-53

Classical & Opera	48-50	Pop, Rock & Indie	51
Jazz & Blues	50	Theatre & Performance	52

Eating and Drinking · 54-63

British restaurants	54-55	Global/American restaurants	60-62
European & Asian restaurants	56-60	Bars	63

Retail Therapy · 64-73

Shopping Centres	64-68	Speciality Markets	69-73

Manchester's Quarters · 74-83

Gay Manchester · 84-89

Parks and Gardens · 90-97

Out into the Countryside · 98-105

Where to Stay · 106-107

Hotels	106-107	Travel Accommodation	107
B&B and Guest Houses	107		

Other useful information · 111-114

Map	111-113	Travel Information	114

4
Manchester

Inviting, original, edgy, happening, different: spend any time in Manchester and you'll soon see it's a place like no other.

This free-spirited city demands your attention with a warm, no-nonsense welcome and a liberating open-mindedness that challenges you to take part.

Manchester has thrown off its grimy industrial image for good and reinvented itself as a truly contemporary metropolis, with modern landmark buildings, a brilliant source of art and culture, great bars and world-class hospitality.

Bring your ideas, your energy and your attitude to Manchester, and you'll fit right in – that's what makes this city uniquely Manchester...

Cityscapes

Manchester is a dramatic mix of old and new. The futuristic design and innovative shapes of its contemporary architecture sit side by side with the spires and grinning gargoyles of its proud past.

Manchester's Industrial Heritage

As every school child knows, the Industrial Revolution of the 18th and 19th centuries led the world into the modern era. Manchester was the trail-blazing spirit behind the whole event. Transport yourself back in time with the fascinating legacy of a period that changed the way we live.

Manchester's Music

Manchester is one of the world's most innovative and exciting places for both making music and going out to listen to it. This long musical heritage rubs off on the performing arts in general, making Manchester a great place for a cultural night out. Here you can have it all: enjoy world-class classical performances, nibble tapas as you listen to live jazz, follow in the footsteps of Morrissey, or look out for the next Oasis in one of the city's 30-plus intimate live venues.

Museums & Galleries

From classical masterpieces to cutting-edge modern works, from a history of bats to a tour of the world's most famous football club, Greater Manchester's museums and galleries offer a world-class array of delights to interest and inspire.

Food & Drink

Manchester's broad cultural mix adds up to a great range of places to eat and drink. From Michelin-style gourmet to fresh local produce at speciality markets – from stylish venues for intimate occasions to out-of-the-way places for a good, cheap meal with friends – there's good food a plenty in Manchester.

Shopping

Manchester does funky, fashionable, chic and sleek better than anywhere else in the country. Retail therapy is the city's speciality. Hunt down something unique at Saturday's Tib Street fashion market, browse for vintage chic and rare records in the Northern Quarter, or cruise the designer stores and then relax with a long lunch and cocktails in the Harvey Nichols Brasserie.

Manchester's People

The people of Manchester have an attitude to life and a way of doing things all their own. They're an easy, self-deprecating lot with a wicked sense of humour and an appetite for adventure (and a party). But don't be fooled: behind that engaging, easy-going exterior there lies ambition and desire for change. Hardly surprising Manchester is such a proud, forward-thinking city.

6
Manchester

Want More Information?
For accommodation availability, bookings or information on the many attractions in and around the city:
Visit www.visitmanchester.com Manchester's official tourism website
Call: +44 (0) 871 222 8223
Email: touristinformation@marketing-manchester.co.uk

7
Manchester

When you're in Manchester visit our Tourist Information Centre
in the City Centre:

Manchester Visitor Information Centre
Town Hall Extension
Lloyd Street, Manchester, M60 2LA

Chinese Arts Centre

The Chinese Arts Centre offers changing contemporary arts exhibitions, workshops, education programmes and information or Chinese art and culture. It also has a library and artist database.

ℹ Thomas St,
Manchester M4 1EU

T (0161) 832 7271

www.chinese-arts-centre.org

❋ Opening times vary;
please phone

Reinvention

Manchester is home to the second largest Chinese community in the UK, and the Chinese Arts Centre is located in the regenerated Northern Quarter, Manchester's creative heart. The centre stages exhibitions of contemporary visual arts from a broad variety of media; areas include architecture, design, fashion, installation, painting, photography, printmaking, sculpture, and video, as well as cross-artform work. The exhibition programme consists of a combination of solo and group shows. The building successfully links Manchester's 19th-century past as an economic powerhouse and the originator of the Industrial Revolution, with its overall regeneration and reinvention as a creative city.

Feng Shui

Chinese-inspired elements include imported antique Chinese doors, special banners that channel positive Feng Shui, and the use of colour inspired by architectural landmarks such as Beijing's Forbidden City. The flooring in the gallery has been inspired by Hutong housing, a traditional type of courtyard house, synonymous with Beijing, which is now being lost to redevelopment. There is further Chinese detailing including the use of rich woods with traditional treatments, lacquers, columns and stylised motifs throughout the building. A full height black zinc wall, visible from outside, contains a three-metre-long linear strip housing a goldfish tank. The colours o the nine swimming fish provide a vivid flash of colour against the zinc, and goldfish are a potent symbol of good fortune and prosperity in the Chinese community worldwide.

★ Highlights
Architectural motifs
125 sqm Primary Gallery
Teahouse

ℹ Information
🍴 Shop, teahouse
♿ Good
£ Admission prices vary according to exhibition
+ Special exhibitions

rich woods
with
traditional
treatments

Manchester's lively centre for international cinema and visual arts. Its three galleries exhibit contemporary art, sculpture and photography, while three cinema screens show a wide variety of independent films. There is also a café, a bookshop and a bar.

i 70 Oxford Road,
Manchester M1 5NH

T (0161) 200 1500

www.cornerhouse.org

※ Daily 11-11

Artistic Excellence
Cornerhouse is one of the UK's leading centres for film and visual arts. Since opening in 1985 it has achieved an international reputation for artistic excellence and innovation. Contemporary art galleries and three cinema screens are ranged over three floors, along with a bar, café and bookshop. The centre also operates Cornerhouse Publications, an international distribution service for visual arts books and catalogues.

Independent Cinema
Cornerhouse is a flagship independent film theatre. On average, 35 titles are screened across the three screens each month. The programme is international in scope and offers new and innovative film and video alongside more familiar work, shown within the context of the history of world cinema. This results in the screening of a very wide range of

work, including new and re-releases; second runs of overlooked or underrated titles; repertory and 'classic' films; archive material; short films and videos; animation; documentary film and video; avant garde film; and European or foreign language films.

The Galleries
Cornerhouse galleries bring the best in contemporary visual arts to the city, exhibiting work of international significance and receiving touring exhibitions. The programme provides a launch pad for young artists as well as exhibiting established British and foreign artists through a balance of solo and themed exhibitions, retrospectives and the commissioning of new work. In addition to the formal exhibition programme, Cornerhouse Visual Arts Department also organise a wide range of one-off events.

★ Highlights
Wide scope of independent films
Innovative one-off exhibitions
Dedicated visual arts bookshop

i Information
🍽 Bookshop, café, bar
♿ Good
£ Cinema admission £5.20/£3.70; free admission to galleries
+ Special exhibitions

eputation
or artistic
xcellence

CORNERHOUSE
MONSOON
WEDDING

flagship
independent
film theatre

10
Gallery of Costume

Have you ever wondered what Victorian women wore for cycling or playing tennis? Can you guess the connection between a wetsuit and a 1980s clubbing outfit? For answers, delve into the Gallery of Costume's collection of 20,000 items of clothing.

ℹ Platt Hall, Wilmslow Road, Manchester M14 5LL

T (0161) 224 5217

www.manchestergalleries.org

✳ Last Sat of month 10-5, or by appointment

Platt Hall
Housed in the elegant surroundings of Platt Hall, an 18th-century textile merchant's home, the Gallery of Costume is home to one of the largest collections of clothing and fashion accessories in the UK, amounting to more than 20,000 items. The gallery is open by appointment to pre-booked groups and researchers, Tues-Fri 10-12 and 1-5.

Designer Wear to Weavers' Clogs
The collection contains clothes worn by men, women and children from the 17th century to the present day. Many of the clothes represent high fashion of the day. Other, much rarer items represent the basic but equally interesting dress of working people, such as the clogs and shawls of Lancashire weavers. The Gallery continues to collect all kinds of clothes worn by people in Britain, including contemporary designer wear, sports and leisure clothes, underwear and the fashions of Manchester's South Asian communities.

Clothes as Identity
Because of the vast size of the collection, only a small percentage of the total collection can be on display at any one time. However, you can explore the costume collections further by browsing the themes listed on the gallery's website. Among other things, the themes explore the cult of the designer – an obsession that gathered strength and momentum during the 20th century – and the different kinds of clothes we wear as visual emblems to define formal or informal occasions. The constant recycling of fashions is also explored, as is the way we use clothes as a means of defining sexuality and identity.

⭐ Highlights
Workers' clothing
Designer gear
Materials and Making
Underwear

ℹ Information
🍴 Shop
♿ Good
£ Free admission
+ Special exhibitions

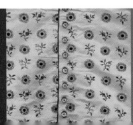

the cult of the designer

clogs and shawls of Lancashire weavers

Britain's only museum dedicated to hats and the hatting industry, with a comprehensive range of visitor facilities. Top hats, bowler hats, trilbies, homburgs, synthetic hats from the 1960s – Hat Works has them all, along with hat-making machinery, demonstrations and audio-visual theatres.

ℹ Wellington Mill, Wellington Road South, Stockport SK3 0EU

T (0161) 355 7770

www.hatworks.org.uk

❈ Mon-Fri 10-5, Sat-Sun 1-5

The Hatting Industry

The ground floor provides an introduction to fur felt hat-making, which began to concentrate in the Stockport area from the 17th century. A farmer, making hats to supplement his income, is shown preparing fur to be shaped into hats. The bubbling, steaming kettle into which the hats were dipped is a memorable part of every visit to the museum. Visitors can also walk through the back kitchen of a small terraced house to see how a worker in a hat factory might have lived in the late 19th century, when hatting became an urban occupation.

The Machinery Collection

Hat Works has a unique collection of hatting machinery. With approximately 45 different processes going into making one hat, the mechanical variety at Hat Works is astounding. A tour round Hat Works' ground floor allows the visitor to see most of the machines in the museum's collection. They sift and clean fur, shape hats, shrink hats, stiffen and dye hats, bend brims and trim hats. Many of them still work, and demonstrators are on hand to start them up. Also on display is a comprehensive selection of hand tools used in hat making.

Hat Block Making

One of the most atmospheric parts of the museum is the recreation of a hat block maker's workshop and office. A labyrinth of lathes with a web of leather driving belts still function, and the old-fashioned office, complete with desk diary and cigarette packet, is in as much orderly chaos as it used to be.

★ Highlights
Hatter's Cottage
Machinery demonstrations
Hat Block Maker's Workshop

ℹ Information
🍽 Internet café, gift shop
♿ Excellent
£ Free admission
+ Guided tours

Top hats, bowler hats, trilbies

homburgs, synthetic hats, felt hats

12

Imperial War Museum North

The Imperial War Museum North explores how people's lives are shaped by war and conflict, while the building itself is an attraction in its own right: the concept for the architecture was a globe, shattered by conflict and then reassembled on the site.

ℹ The Quays, Trafford Wharf Road, Trafford Park, Manchester M17 1TZ

T (0161) 836 4000

www.iwm.org.uk/north

✺ Daily 10-6

Shattered Globe

One of the most celebrated museums in Britain today, Imperial War Museum North is about people and their stories – about how lives have been, and still are, shaped by war and conflict. The award-winning building by international architect Daniel Libeskind is a symbol of our world torn apart by conflict and is situated at The Quays, a waterfront destination two miles from Manchester city centre.

The Big Picture

Imperial War Museum North uses thought-provoking and innovative display techniques such as the Big Picture, which puts you right in the centre of the experience by using a dramatic display of projected images and sound. The Main Exhibition Space also houses thousands of exhibits, from a T34 Russian tank and Harrier jump-jet to clothing, diaries and works of art, as well as a series of interactive Action Stations. 'Time Line' explores the history of conflict in the 20th and 21st centuries, featuring key landmark events involving British and Commonwealth citizens. Built into the walls of two of the silos, 'Time Stacks' contains themed trays of objects which can be handled by visitors.

Daily Tours

In addition to the above, the varied exhibition and events programme at the Imperial War Museum North offers activities for adults and families, daily tours and object-handling sessions.

★ Highlights
The Big Picture
Action Stations
'TimeStacks'
Silos

ℹ Information
🍴 Restaurant, café
♿ Excellent
£ Free admission
+ Guided tours

THE TANK

14 Manchester Airport Aviation Viewing Park

A fun family day out, with the chance to take a close look at the flagship of the Concorde fleet, which is parked up on a replica runway. There's a visitor centre, an aviation classroom, and a viewing park with picnic tables and great views of the planes as they come in to land.

i Manchester Airport,
Manchester M90 1QX

T (0161) 904 7460

www.manchesterairport.co.uk

❋ Daily 8.30-dusk

Concorde

The star attraction within the Viewing Park is the G-BOAC Concorde, the first Concorde to go on public display in Britain. In 2004 the aircraft was moved to a replica runway in the Aviation Viewing Park and unveiled for public display. Millions of passengers can now look down on Concorde as they fly in and out of Britain's third busiest airport. For a closer look, take an extended technical tour on board the flagship of the Concorde fleet, or peer down the 'nose' of the aircraft from a newly extended viewing mound. Those truly enamoured of Concorde can even get married in the rear cabin!

Visitor Centre and Viewing Park

The forward section of a retired Monarch Airlines DC-10 has been converted into an 'aviation classroom', complete with aircraft interior, cockpit and audio-visual kit. Also on display is an Avro RJX, the last civil airliner built in the UK. Meanwhile, the Aviation Viewing Park provides great views of planes taking off and landing, along with picnic sites, refreshments, toilets and a small visitor centre. There is also an aviation shop, which sells a wide range of aviation merchandise, gifts and Concorde memorabilia. The rest of the site is a thriving habitat for wildlife, and everything is wheelchair or pushchair accessible.

★ Highlights
Concorde
Avro RJX
Aviation classroom

i Information	
🍴	Restaurants, cafés, bars
♿	Excellent
£	£3 per car inc. driver, plus £1 for each additional passenger
+	Guided tours

flagship of the Concorde fleet

an aviation classroom

Manchester Art Gallery

The recently revamped Manchester Art Gallery houses one of the world's finest collections of art, displayed in spectacular surroundings. There are also fun interactive exhibits and special exhibitions to enjoy.

i Manchester Airport,
Manchester M90 1QX

T (0161) 904 7460

www.manchesterairport.co.uk

❀ Daily 8.30-dusk

200-year History
Manchester Art Gallery is home to the city's world-class art collection, developed over 200 years and still growing. Founded as the Royal Manchester Institution in 1823, the building and its collections were handed over to the city in 1882 to become the Manchester Art Gallery. A brand new extension, unveiled in 2002, has doubled the display space, and the gallery now holds more than 25,000 objects of fine art, decorative art and costume.

Fine Art
The gallery showcases nearly 13,000 items, including painting, sculpture, drawings, watercolours, prints, posters and photographs. The collection is best known for its world-famous Pre-Raphaelite paintings by artists such as Holman Hunt and

Dante Gabriel Rossetti. The collection also includes British and European art from the 17th century right up to the present day, from L S Lowry to David Hockney and Terence Conran. The permanent displays also cover the emergence of Romanticism, with the work of some of our best-known artists – JMW Turner, John Constable and William Blake.

Decorative Art
There's a huge craft and design collection to explore, from ceramics, glass and furniture to metalwork, wallpaper and dolls houses. Highlights include early English slipware, 17th-century silver, and a growing collection of contemporary furniture and lighting design.

★ Highlights
Victorian Gallery
Pre-Raphaelite Collection
Modern and Contemporary Galleries

i Information	
🍴	Shop, café
♿	Excellent
£	Free admission
+	Special exhibitions

world-famous pre-Raphaelite paintings

16
Manchester Cathedral

Manchester Cathedral sports a gorgeous interior with the finest late-medieval woodwork in the North – the choir and the ceiling, in particular, are bursting with life in their carved details. The cathedral is a venue for services including evensong and concerts.

i Manchester Cathedral,
Victoria Street,
Manchester M3 1SX

T (0161) 833 2220

www.manchestercathedral.org

❀ Please phone for details

Church to Cathedral
At one time, the 'Parish Church of Manchester' marked the epicentre of medieval Manchester, though much of the cathedral's present-day exterior is a 19th-century reconstruction by Joseph Crowther. The highlight is undoubtedly the detailed 15th-century woodwork carried out by the highly skilled 'Ripon Carvers'.

New Visitors' Centre
With its new refectory and visitors' centre, Manchester Cathedral is now an essential sight for visitors to the city. An exhibition containing interactive displays offers an insight into medieval Manchester, local history and the developing role of the Cathedral itself.

The Hanging Bridge
One of the cathedral's finest features is the historic Hanging Bridge, a 15th-century structure that once connected the medieval town with the church. The bridge is mentioned in many medieval documents and was a prominent feature of old Manchester. Built in 1421, the bridge has been excavated and can now be viewed – indeed touched – in the basement restaurant.

The Angel Stone
Presently mounted to the left of the Pulpitum Screen, the Angel Stone is a fragment of a Saxon church, possibly dating back as far as AD 700. The Saxon words inscribed on the stone mean 'Into thy hands, O Lord, I commend my spirit'. It is thought that there may have been a timber church dating back to early Saxon times on the original cathedral site.

★ Highlights
Choir carved by the 'Ripon Carvers'
The Hanging Bridge
The Angel Stone

_i_ Information	
🍴	Restaurant, café
♿	Few
£	Free admission
+	Gardens on site

18 Manchester City Football Club

Manchester City's new home, the City of Manchester Stadium, is one of the most spectacular sporting arenas in the country. It also doubles as a venue for a variety of uses. For the best overview, take the Manchester City Experience Tour.

ℹ️ City of Manchester Stadium,
Sportcity, Eastlands,
Manchester M11 3FF

☎ (0161) 231 3200

www.mcfc.co.uk

✳️ Mon-Sat 9.30-4.30, Sun 11-3, closed match days

125 years of Football

The Manchester City Experience (Museum & Stadium Tour) combines the rich sporting history of Manchester City Football Club with a 60-minute tour of the awe-inspiring City of Manchester Stadium, which was created for the 2002 Commonwealth Games. The Experience begins at the club museum, which encapsulates its 125-year history and the fanaticism that it has inspired. You can try your hand at being the next John Motson by commentating on glorious goals from City's past, relive the greatest moments on the Video Jukebox, or simply spend your time examining some of the club's extensive memorabilia. Dedicated displays include Maine Road 1923-2003, City's Kits, the FA Cup Story, League Championship Glory, Cult Players, European Success, Derby Day, The Managers, and Fan City. There are also a number of interactive displays – including a virtual tour of Maine Road – and Dream Team, where you can pick your best City XI of all time.

Tour the Stadium

If you prefer, soak up the atmosphere with a behind-the-scenes tour of the City of Manchester Stadium. Your guide will give you an insight into the day-to-day activities of the club, allowing you to glimpse what really goes on. Walk in the footsteps of favourite players down by the pitch or admire the grandeur of the building from one of the executive lounges. The tour includes visits to the Box Level, the Corporate Lounge, the Directors' Box, Dressing Room, the Walk of Pride (players' tunnel), warm-up room, press facilities, the pitch side and dugouts.

★ Highlights

Commentary Box
Video Jukebox
Dream Team

ℹ️ Information

🍽️ Restaurant, café
♿ Excellent
£ £8.75/£4.75, family ticket (for 5 people) £25
+ Guided tours

pick your best City XI of all time

Manchester Craft & Design Centre

A spacious, flood-lit oasis in Manchester's Northern Quarter, packed with original pieces of art, craft and design – all of it for sale. The centre comprises 18 studios and hosts an ongoing programme of unusual exhibitions.

ℹ 17 Oak St, Manchester M4 5JD

www.craftanddesign.com

T (0161) 832 4274

❈ Mon-Sat 10-5.30

Artistic Hub

Manchester Craft and Design Centre is a unique organisation comprising 18 retail/studio spaces, an excellent café and a rolling programme of exhibitions from leading national and international craftspeople. Located in Manchester city centre's Northern Quarter, Manchester Craft and Design Centre is at the hub of a growing innovative and artistic community. It is one of the few places in the UK open to the public where contemporary goods are both individually produced and sold on the premises.

18 Studios

Formerly the Smithfield Victorian fish market and crowned with a huge glass roof, the Centre now houses two floors of shops ranging from jewellery, ceramics and textiles to furniture and clothing design. The craftspeople occupying the Centre's 18 studios produce stunning ranges of jewellery, sculpture, clothing, furniture, and much more, in an enormous variety of materials, including wood, metal, plastics, ceramics and textiles.

Creatures and Couches

Exhibitions are ongoing. Previous highlights include the recent Creature Show, which looked at modern-day soft toys and textile works with individual but endearing personalities, and the Sitting Room, a quirky exhibition dedicated to the art of sitting and reading.

★ Highlights
Artists at work
Quirky exhibitions
The café

ℹ Information
🍽 Café
♿ Good
£ Free admission
+ Special exhibitions

rolling
programme
of
exhibitions

spacious
flood-lit
oasis

Manchester Museum

The Manchester Museum houses around six million specimens and objects, from a 200-million-year-old tree fossil to the skeleton of a sperm whale. Kids of all ages will love the chance to examine ancient mummies, reconstructed skeletons of dinosaurs and hundreds of huge creepy-crawlies.

i The University, Oxford Road, Manchester M13 9PL

T (0161) 275 2634

www.museum.man.ac.uk

❀ Tues-Sat 10-5, Sun-Mon 11-4

Six Million Exhibits
Owned by the University of Manchester, and housed in an extension of Alfred Waterhouse's purpose-built natural history galleries of 1888, the Manchester Museum now holds around six million exhibits. The collections were acquired from every corner of the globe, and are split evenly between the humanities and natural sciences.

Mummies and Dinosaurs
The museum has a particularly strong collection of artefacts from ancient Egypt, including mummies and funerary masks. The zoological collections are vast, too: the highlight is probably a cast of a fossilised Tyrannosaurus rex (named 'Stan') from South Dakota. Live animals from the research collection (mainly frogs and lizards) can be seen in the Vivarium.

Long History
The extent of the museum's collection was fuelled by the wealth created by Manchester's international trade in textiles from the late 18th century onwards. The first collections were assembled by the Manchester Society of Natural History, formed in 1821, and in 1850 the collections of the Manchester Geological and Mining Society were added. Today, a changing cross-section of the full collection is on display to visitors, covering everything from native art, fossils and stuffed animals to plants, coins and minerals.

★ Highlights
Ancient mummies
Skeleton of a sperm whale
Tyrannosaurus rex
Vivarium

i Information
⑩ Shop, café, picnic area
♿ Excellent
£ Free admission
+ Special exhibitions

a fossilised T Rex named Stan

22

Manchester Town Hall

This magnificent building was designed in neo-Gothic style by Alfred Waterhouse (also responsible for the Natural History Museum)

i Albert Square, Manchester M60 2LA

T (0161) 234 5000

www.manchester.gov.uk

✿ Mon-Fri 9-5

Eight-tonne Abel

The most prominent feature is the 85m-tall bell tower, which houses eight bells, including eight-tonne 'Great Abel' – named after the acting mayor on the building's completion in 1877. Though designed to resemble 13th-century English Gothic architecture, the building nevertheless included innovative technologies, such as a warm air heating system.

Great Hall

Head for the Great Hall to catch sight of the 12 murals by celebrated Pre-Raphaelite painter Ford Maddox Brown. On the floor you'll notice mosaics of bees and cotton flowers – both of which symbolise Manchester's industry. Look up to the ceiling and you'll notice a series of panels, each depicting the coats of arms of the cities and nations that Manchester traded with in the past. Fourteen million bricks and 4,000 square metres of marble went into the construction of the Town Hall, making it one of the most expensive buildings in England at the time of its construction.

Tours

The Town Hall's main entrance is guarded by a statue of Agricola, the Roman general who founded Manchester in AD 79, while the exterior is adorned with further statues of historical figures. Tours of the building take place every Saturday (phone to arrange in advance), though visitors are welcome to explore on their own throughout the week.

★ Highlights
The Great Hall
Ford Maddox Brown Murals
The Bell Tower
Statue of Agricola

i Information	
🍽	Restaurant, café
♿	Excellent
£	Free except for special exhibitions
+	Guided tours

24 Manchester United Football Club

Nicknamed the 'Theatre of Dreams', Old Trafford is acknowledged by many to be the ultimate football stadium. The popular 'Museum and Tour' details the history of the club from 1878 to the present day, and enables visitors to get right behind the scenes.

i Sir Matt Busby Way,
Old Trafford, Manchester
M16 0RA

T 0870 442 1994

www.manutd.com
Daily 9.30-5

Theatre of Dreams

Old Trafford is the largest club football ground in Britain, with a capacity of 76,000 – making it one of the most atmospheric and historic stadiums in the world. Given the nickname 'Theatre of Dreams' by Sir Bobby Charlton, it has played host to some of the best players, teams and football contests over the course of almost 100 years. The stadium became Manchester United's home in 1910, but suffered extensive damage when it was bombed during World War II. The Reds relocated to Manchester City's Maine Road stadium until the rebuilding of Old Trafford was completed in 1949.

Museum and Tour

Relive the club's triumphs, tragedies and trophies at the Manchester United Museum. Follow the history of the club from 1878 to the present day, including the Hall of Fame and Roll of Honour. Split over three floors, the museum covers every detail of United's story, including the full array of trophies, from youth team silverware won by the Busby Babes to bigger prizes like the European Cup. Delve behind the scenes at the Theatre of Dreams by taking the Stadium Tour. Stand in Sir Alex Ferguson's spot in the dugout, sit in the home changing room at your favourite player's peg, and emerge from the player's tunnel to the roar of the crowd.

★ Highlights
Hall of Fame
Trophy Room
North Stand
Dressing Room

i Information
🍽 Restaurant, café
♿ Excellent
£ Museum and tour £9.50/£6.50, family ticket £27
+ Guided tours

26 Museum of Science & Industry

The Museum of Science and Industry is based on the site of the oldest passenger railway station in the world. The huge site has five historic buildings packed with fascinating exhibits, hands-on galleries, historic working machinery and superb special exhibitions.

i Liverpool Road, Castlefield, Manchester M3 4FP

T (0161) 832 2244

www.msim.org.uk

☀ Daily 10-5

A World First

Explore the history, science and industry of Manchester and its people through the museum's galleries, which tell the story of the world's first industrial city. Each of the five historic buildings provides an inspiring setting for the permanent displays and special exhibitions. Whether you enjoy historic working machinery, scientific instruments, the nostalgic appeal of old household appliances or getting your hands on interactive exhibits, you should find a gallery to suit you.

Xperiment

Explore the wonders of science in Xperiment – a hands-on science gallery full of interactive exhibits that will captivate enquiring minds of all ages. Stimulate your brain in the Mind Maze, test the senses, reveal the magic of materials and experiment with energy.

You'll get the chance to examine a giant eyeball, lift a car or experience a tornado being formed. There's also a Discovery Den for the under-5s.

Holodecks and Cameras

For 200 years Manchester has been a hotbed of scientific discovery and innovation. Learn how local scientists, both past and present, have shaped the modern world. Four audio-visual 'holodecks' bring science to life by immersing you in the fascinating worlds of John Dalton, James Joule, Ernest Rutherford and Sir Bernard Lovell. Elsewhere in the museum, learn how Richard Beard opened Manchester's first photographic studio (in 1841), and how locals set up businesses to exploit the growing interest in photography. You can also see J T Chapman's innovative dry photographic plates, which he sold under the brand name 'Manchester'.

★ Highlights
MarsQuest
Morphis simulator
Xperiment
Reconstructed Victorian sewer
Planetarium

i Information	
†O†	Restaurant, café
&	Very good
£	Free except for special exhibitions
+	Special exhibitions

Ordsall Hall Museum

Ordsall Hall is a wonderfully preserved black-and-white timbered manor house – one of England's finest examples of Tudor architecture. A visit to the museum takes you straight back to the late 16th century, complete with a fully furnished Great Hall and an exhibition with interactive displays.

i 322 Ordsall Lane, Ordsall, Salford M5 3AN

T (0161) 872 0251

www.salford.gov.uk/ordsallhall

❋ Mon-Fri 10-4, Sun 1-4

Tudor Gem
Once home to the wealthy Radclyffe family, and dating back more than eight centuries, Ordsall Hall is one of the finest examples of Tudor architecture in the region. The ground floor of the black-and-white timbered hall is set out as a period manor house of the late 16th century, complete with Great Hall, Star Chamber and Kitchen. Upstairs is the changing exhibition area with a range of interactive shows and displays.

Guy Fawkes Connection
The earliest records of Ordsall Hall date back to 1177, when 'Ordeshala' first appeared in print. The manor house passed into the hands of the Radclyffe family in around 1335, and it was sometime after this date that the hall was enlarged. Several centuries later, according to local legend, Guy Fawkes hatched his plot to blow up the Houses of Parliament while staying here.

Ghosts and Tudor Trends
Wander back through time and soak up the atmosphere of the fully furnished Great Hall and Star Chamber bedroom. Get the low-down on Tudor lifestyles, see what's cooking in the Kitchen, or unearth the wealth of new discoveries to be made in the exciting family events and exhibitions programme. Before you leave, don't forget to check out the ghost camera – who knows, you may be lucky enough to catch footage of one of Ordsall Hall's resident ghosts?

★ Highlights
Great Hall
Star Chamber
Ghost camera

i Information
🍴 Shop
♿ Moderate
£ Free admission
+ Special exhibitions

check out
the ghost
camera

People's History Museum

Housed in a former Edwardian pumping station on the banks of the River Irwell, the People's History Museum is the only museum dedicated to the working people of Britain. The museum follows the story of how working people joined forces to change society, improving life for future generations.

ℹ The Pump House, Bridge Street, Manchester M3 3ER

☎ (0161) 839 6061

www.phm.org.uk

❀ Tues-Sun 11-4.30

Footballers and Suffragettes

The museum offers a unique look at the lives of ordinary working people over the last 200 years, from Victorian cotton workers to professional footballers. The galleries take visitors through scenes such as the Peterloo massacre in Manchester, a secret trade union meeting, sweatshop work in an attic room and a suffragettes' kitchen. The richness of working people's lives is illustrated through the museum's collections of banners, photographs, badges, posters, ephemera, tools, regalia, paintings and everyday objects.

The Collections

The museum holds the largest collection of historic trade union and political banners in the world and is the UK's leading authority on the conservation and study of banners. There are nearly 400 banners in the collection, including the world's oldest trade union banner – that of the Liverpool Tinplate Workers of 1821. In 1990 the Labour Party archives were transferred to the museum, followed by the collections of the Communist Party of Great Britain. Since then, the museum has broadened the range of material it collects to cover the wider social history of all working people.

Family Fun

Interactive displays, developed especially with families in mind, are located throughout the main galleries. Have fun creating your own badge, shopping at a 1930s Co-op, performing your own Punch & Judy Show, cooperating to build an arch, recording your opinions, producing a fuzzy felt banner and more. The museum lays on a comprehensive programme of events throughout the year, including school holidays. These are often related to the changing exhibitions and include activities for families as well as adults.

★ Highlights
Interactive displays
Trade union banners
Suffragettes' kitchen

ℹ Information	
🍽	Shop, café
♿	Excellent
£	Free admission
+	Special exhibitions

the richness of working people's lives

30 Salford Museum & Art Gallery

Salford Museum & Art Gallery features an authentic period street from 1890, complete with shops and houses. New to the museum is the Lifetimes Gallery, which showcases Salford's past and present. Meanwhile, the Victorian Gallery features sculptures, paintings, pottery, furniture and decorative arts.

i Peel Park, The Crescent, Salford, M5 4WU

T (0161) 778 0800

www.salford.gov.uk/salfordmuseum

❋ Mon-Fri 10-4.45, Sat-Sun 1-5

Recreated Victorian Street and Gallery

Many original shop fronts feature in a wonderful recreation of a typical Northern street at the end of the 19th century and brought to life with authentic sounds. Visit the Blue Lion Pub, marvel at the pills and potions in the chemist's window, and compare the home comforts of the Victorian parlour to the worker's cottage. Then relax amid the splendour (and clutter) of Victorian times by visiting the Gallery, where the Victorians' passion for painting, pottery and fine furniture is in evidence. Alternatively, get stuck in at the new Lifetimes Gallery, with its hands-on exhibits, listening points and IT zone.

Temporary Exhibitions

Enjoy a varied and lively programme of temporary exhibitions, ranging from contemporary art and crafts, archaeology and architecture, to documentary photography and social history. Recent exhibitions include the story of Salford's textile industry, with a focus on the working life in mills and cottage industries across the region.

Events and Activities

The museum also lays on a whole range of hands-on activities for all the family. Try out one of the many games or quizzes, or get to grips with some unusual art materials in a creative art session. There's drama, dance and music too. A full family-friendly programme runs during school holidays.

★ Highlights
Recreated 1890s street
Chemist and Druggist Shop
Artisan's Cottage
Victorian Gallery

i Information
🍴 Shop, café
♿ Excellent
£ Free
+ Special exhibitions

the home comforts of the Victorian parlour

32
The Lowry

A stunning landmark, The Lowry captures that unusual combination of functionality and beauty, as stainless steel and gla merge with water and light. Along with cafés, bars and a restaurant, the complex provides an extraordinary backdrop for the visual and performing arts.

i The Lowry, Pier 8, Salford
Quays M50 3AZ

T 0870 787 5780

www.thelowry.com

✳ Tue-Sat 10-8, Sun-Mon 10-6

Architectural Landmark

The Lowry opened its doors in April 2000, bringing together a wide variety of performing and visual arts under one roof. Set in a magnificent waterside location at the heart of the redeveloped Salford Quays in Greater Manchester, The Lowry is an architectural flagship with a unique and dynamic identity. Rising from the regenerated docklands, it is a welcoming building, designed to reflect the surrounding waterways in its glass and metallic surfaces.

Performing and Visual Arts

The Lowry houses two main theatres and a studio space for the performing arts, presenting a full range of drama, opera, ballet, dance, musicals, children's shows, popular music, jazz, folk, comedy and gallery space. The latter houses the works of L S Lowry alongside contemporary exhibitions

Waterside Views

The layout of The Lowry encourages visitors to explore and enjoy the variety of facilities housed within it throughout the day and evening. An open, ramped route with dramatic views connects the theatre foyers ar gallery spaces, forming a public promenade around the building, linking all activities. Cafés, bars and restaurant are situated along the southern side of the building, with spectacular waterside views. In fine weather, the quayside terraces come into play, overlooking the expansive Manchester Ship Canal.

★ Highlights
L S Lowry Collection
Quayside terraces
Lyric Theatre

i Information
🍽 Restaurant, cafés, bars
♿ Excellent
£ Gallery admission free; theatre admission varies
+ Special exhibitions

34
Urbis

Located in the heart of Manchester, Urbis is an exhibition centre dedicated to city life, featuring interactive exhibits and dynamic changing exhibitions which explore the people, place and pulse of the modern city, both here in Manchester and around the globe.

i Cathedral Gardens, Manchester
M4 3BG

T (0161) 605 8200

www.urbis.org.uk

❀ Tues-Sun 10-6

Go Global

Urbis is a new kind of museum set in a dramatic glass building rising high above the centre of Manchester. Interactive exhibits lead you on a journey exploring life in different cities around the world. Urbis focuses especially on the cities of Los Angeles, Manchester, Paris, Sao Paulo, Singapore and Tokyo. Your visit to Urbis begins with a one minute sky glide in The MEN Glass Elevator. With the city as backdrop, you can then explore the four cascading exhibition floors at your own pace. Using the interactive exhibits, you can create your own identity card, take a ride through different world cities, or go global to discover a 3D satellite view of any city on the planet with the help of an interactive version of Google

Earth. There's also a dynamic programme of changing exhibitions offering unique insights into the culture of the modern city, with innovative explorations of design, architecture, graffiti, music and the urban environment.

Evolution of the City

Explore how people change, and are changed by, the city they call 'home'. Experience 200 years of Manchester' history through two unique multi-sensory theatres, 'Time' and 'Place'. Step into the lives of the people you meet with an interactive, special effects journey through their home cities: see Singapore by taxi and hang out at a street-side café in Sao Paulo.

★ Highlights
Dramatic glass structure
3D satellite views of world cities
Sky glide in the MEN Glass Elevator
Manchester Exhibition Floor

i Information
🍴 Restaurant, café
♿ Good
£ Free except for special exhibitions
+ Special exhibitions

Whitworth Art Gallery

Set behind an Edwardian facade, with a light and spacious modern interior, the Whitworth Art Gallery is home to a famous collection of British watercolours, modern and historic prints, drawings, paintings and sculptures, textiles and wallpapers.

i University of Manchester,
Oxford Road,
Manchester M15 6ER

T (0161) 275 7450

www.whitworth.man.ac.uk

❀ Mon-Sat 10-5, Sun 2-5

Art on a Small Scale

The Whitworth Art Gallery is home to an impressive range of watercolours, prints, drawings, modern art and sculpture, as well as the largest collections of textiles and wallpapers outside London. The collection is particularly strong in works on a small scale, such as drawings, prints and textiles. Several of the exhibition galleries are specially designed for displays of this kind of work and have an intimate feel to them. Meanwhile, the Mezzanine Court and the South Gallery (with its views of Whitworth Park) are both light, airy spaces used for the display of larger works.

Tours and Workshops

The Whitworth uses its collections to create ever-changing exhibitions exploring different themes. The gallery also hosts a programme of innovative touring exhibitions, and curators are happy to provide access to reserve collections, especially for study purposes. A selection of tours, lectures, practical workshops and concerts accompanies the exhibition programme. For a general introduction to the Whitworth Art Gallery and its collections, try the Eyeopener Tour, which takes place every Saturday at 2pm.

The Textile Gallery

The newly refurbished Textile Gallery displays fabrics from around the world. It has a fun hands-on resource, which includes children's costumes for dressing up and different fabrics to touch and compare. There is also a range of textile-related art materials for help with weaving, or designing costumes for your very own finger puppet.

★ Highlights
Eyeopener Tour
Wallpapers and textiles
Genesis, by Jacob Epstein

i Information	
❙❙	Shop, café
♿	Good
£	Free admission
+	Special exhibitions

Admission prices for the following museums and attractions are graded according to the price of a single adult admission:
£ = under £5; ££ = £5-£10; £££ = over £10

⭐ Central Manchester

Astley Green Colliery Museum (free)
See Europe's largest steam winding engine, the magnificent engine house and outdoor displays of industrial artefacts. The lattice construction headgear over the shaft stands 100ft high and is the finest example of its kind in Britain.

ℹ Higher Green Lane, Astley, Tyldesley
T (01942) 708 969
www.agcm.org.uk
❋ Sun 12-5, Tues 1-5, Thurs 1-5

Imperial War Museum North (free)
The Imperial War Museum North explores how people's lives are shaped by war and conflict, while the building itself is an attraction in its own right: the concept for the architecture was a globe, shattered by conflict and then reassembled on the site. See also p.12.

ℹ The Quays, Trafford Wharf Road
T (0161) 836 4000
www.iwm.org.uk/north
❋ March-Oct daily 10-6, Nov-Feb 10-5

Manchester City Football Club (££)
The Manchester City Experience (Museum & Stadium Tour) combines the rich sporting history of Manchester City Football Club with a 60-minute tour of the awe-inspiring City of Manchester Stadium, which was created for the 2002 Commonwealth Games. See also p.18.

ℹ City of Manchester Stadium, Sportcity, Eastlands
T (0161) 231 3200
www.mcfc.co.uk
❋ Mon-Sat 9.30-4.30, Sun 11-3

Manchester Jewish Museum (free)
Manchester's Jewish history is recorded and displayed in this museum, housed in the restored Spanish and Portuguese synagogue. Exhibitions show everyday life in the community back to the 1740s. Hosts an education programme, demonstrations, music and talks.

ℹ 190 Cheetham Hill Road
T (0161) 832 9879
www.manchesterjewishmuseum.com
❋ Mon-Thurs 10.30-4, Sun 11-5

Manchester Museum (free)
The Manchester Museum houses around six million specimens and objects, from a 200-million-year-old tree fossil to the skeleton of a sperm whale. Kids of all ages will love the chance to examine ancient mummies, reconstructed skeletons of dinosaurs and hundreds of huge creepy-crawlies. See also p.20.

ℹ The University, Oxford Road
T (0161) 275 2634
www.museum.man.ac.uk
❋ Tues-Sat 10-5, Sun 11-4

200-million-year-old tree fossil

Manchester Police Museum (free)

Set in a Victorian police station built in 1879, the museum features the development of policing from the Peeler to the present day. There is also a collection of police uniforms from around the world, and a magistrates' court from the late 19th century.

i Newton Street
T (0161) 856 3287
www.gmp.police.uk
❋ Tues 10.30-3.30

Manchester Town Hall (free)

This magnificent building was designed in neo-Gothic style by Alfred Waterhouse and opened in 1877. Amongst its many treasures are the Ford Maddox Brown murals, which are monument to the ideas of Victorian Manchester, portraying science, invention, education, trade and textile industry. See also p.22.

i Albert Square
T (0161) 234 5000
www.manchester.gov.uk
❋ Mon-Fri 9-5

Manchester United Football Club (££)

Nicknamed the 'Theatre of Dreams', Old Trafford is acknowledged by many to be the ultimate football stadium. The popular 'Museum and Tour' details the history of the club from 1878 to the present day, and enables visitors to get right behind the scenes. See also p.24.

i Sir Matt Busby Way, Old Trafford
T 0870 442 1994
www.manutd.com
❋ Daily 9.30-5

Museum of Science and Industry (free/£)

The Museum of Science and Industry is based on the site of the oldest passenger railway station in the world. The huge, 7.5-acre site has five historic buildings packed with fascinating exhibits, hands-on galleries, historic working machinery and superb special exhibitions. See also p.26.

i Liverpool Road, Castlefield
T (0161) 832 2244
www.msim.org.uk
❋ Daily 10-5

People's History Museum (free)

Housed in a former Edwardian pumping station on the banks of the River Irwell, the People's History Museum is the only museum dedicated to the working people of Britain. The museum follows the story of how working people joined forces to change society, improving life for future generations. See also p.29.

i The Pump House, Bridge Street
T (0161) 839 6061
www.phm.org.uk
❋ Tues-Sun 11-4.30

the ultimate football stadium

Museums and Heritage Sites

Urbis (free/£)

Located in the heart of Manchester, Urbis is an exhibition centre dedicated to city life, featuring interactive exhibits and dynamic changing exhibitions which explore the people, place and pulse of the modern city, both here in Manchester and around the globe. See also p.34.

- *i* Cathedral Gardens
- **T** (0161) 605 8200
  www.urbis.org.uk
- ✹ Tues-Sun 10-6

✪ Greater Manchester

Bolton Museum, Art Gallery and Aquarium (free)

A family-friendly museum with a wildlife gallery and activity centre, Egyptian mummies, an aquarium and art gallery. Lays on an innovative programme of changing exhibitions.

- *i* Le Mans Crescent, Bolton
- **T** (01204) 332 211
  www.boltonmuseums.org.uk
- ✹ Mon-Sat 9-5

Bury Art Gallery, Museum & Archive (free)

Home to the Wrigley collection of Victorian art and cutting edge temporary exhibitions. This is also the location of the new Museum & Archive Centre, which traces Bury's history through changing displays and local records.

- *i* Moss Street, Bury
- **T** (0161) 253 5878
  www.bury.gov.uk
- ✹ Tues-Fri 10-5, Sat 10-4.30

Chadkirk Chapel (free)

A beautifully restored 14th-century chapel set in the heart of Chadkirk Country Estate. Learn about the history of this fantastic chapel and its association through legend with the 7th-century missionary St Chad.

- *i* Vale Road, Romiley, Stockport
- **T** (0161) 474 4460
  www.stockport.gov.uk/
  heritageattractions
- ✹ Summer Sat-Sun 1-5,
  winter Sat-Sun 12-4

Corgi Heritage Centre (free)

Discover the fascinating history of the Corgi die-cast model vehicles which gave Corgi a worldwide reputation for excellence. See models on display in the exhibition area and available for sale in the Corgi Classics shop.

- *i* 53 York St, Heywood, Rochdale
- **T** (01706) 627 811
  www.corgi-heritage.co.uk
- ✹ Wed-Sat and Mon 9-5.30

Dunham Massey Hall (££)

A complete country estate with a house, garden and deer park at its centre, Dunham Massey is packed with 300 years of colourful history brought alive by friendly guides, tours, quizzes and imaginative events.

- *i* Dunham Massey, Altrincham
- **T** (0161) 941 1025
  www.nationaltrust.org.uk
- ✹ Apr-Oct Sat–Wed 12-5

300 years of colourful history

Museums and Heritage Sites

Hall i' th' Wood (£)
A typical late-medieval merchant's house and former home of Samuel Crompton, who invented the Spinning Mule. The museum features displays of Crompton's life, his workroom, Lancashire kitchen, oak panelling and Stuart and Georgian furniture.

i Green Way, Bolton
T (01204) 332 370
   www.boltonmuseums.org.uk
Wed-Sun 11-5

Hat Works (free)
The UK's only museum dedicated to hats and the hatting industry, with a comprehensive range of visitor facilities. Top hats, bowler hats, trilbies, homburgs, synthetic hats from the 1960s – Hat Works has them all. See also p.11.

i Wellington Mill, Wellington Road South, Stockport
T (0161) 355 7770
   www.hatworks.org.uk
Mon-Fri 10-5, Sat-Sun 1-5

Horwich Heritage Centre (free)
The centre aims to preserve and present the best of the rich history and heritage of Horwich by featuring specific aspects of Horwich life over the last 100 years through videos, displays, artefacts and exhibits.

i Longworth Road, Horwich, Bolton
T (01204) 847 797
   www.horwichheritage.co.uk
Tues 10-12 and 2-4, Wed 2-4, Fri 10-12 and 2-4, Sat 10-1

Littleborough Coach House & Heritage Centre (free)
A Grade II listed building of architectural and historical interest within an important conservation area. Dating from the late 18th century, it was originally built to serve the Bury horse-drawn coach traffic on the main transport routes into Yorkshire across Blackstone Edge. There are regular exhibitions by local artists, information on local walks and a café selling light lunches.

i Lodge Street, Littleborough, Rochdale
T (01706) 378 481
Opening hours vary; please phone

Museum of the Manchester Regiment (free)
The museum tells the story of the Regiment and its soldiers through 200 years of history, from 1758 until 1958. Enjoy the fine collection of weapons, uniforms and medals and step inside the First World War trench for an experience of what life was like on the Western Front.

i Town Hall, Market Place, Ashton-under-Lyne
T (0161) 342 3710
   www.tameide.gov.uk/museumsandgalleries
Mon-Sat 10-4

step inside
a First
World War
trench

Museum of Transport (£)

The museum has one of the largest transport collections in the country with 90 buses and a small number of other vehicles that represent public transport in the Greater Manchester area, with archives and small exhibits. Special events occur during the year, including a spring and autumn festival, the Heaton Park rally and a special weekend for disabled people.

i Boyle Street, Cheetham

T (0161) 205 2122
www.gmts.co.uk

❀ Sat-Sun and Wed 10-5, winter 10-4

Oldham Museum and Gallery (free)

Situated in a former 'Friends Meeting House', the major new gallery has a programme of changing exhibitions as well as a permanent display ('Going up Town') where visitors can step back in time to the days when the town was dominated by the cotton industry.

i Greaves Street, Oldham

T (0161) 911 4657
www.oldham.gov.uk

❀ Mon-Sat 10-5

Ordsall Hall (free)

Ordsall Hall is a wonderfully preserved black-and-white timbered manor house – one of England's finest examples of Tudor architecture. A visit to the museum takes you straight back to the late 16th century, complete with a fully furnished Great Hall and an exhibition with interactive displays. See also p.28.

i 322 Ordsall Lane, Ordsall, Salford

T (0161) 872 0251
www.salford.gov.uk/ordsallhall

❀ Mon-Fri 10-4, Sun 1-4

Quarry Bank Mill (££)

A working 18th-century water-powered cotton mill set in beautiful National Trust country parkland. Working demonstrations, from hand-spinning and weaving to original mill weaving machines producing cloth for sale in the shop. Restaurant and picnic area.

i Styal Estate, Wilmslow

T (01625) 527 468
www.quarrybankmill.org.uk

❀ Mid Mar-Oct daily 11-5, Nov-mid Mar Wed-Sun 11-4

Rochdale Pioneers Museum (£)

The Rochdale Pioneers Museum is the home of the worldwide co-operative movement. Journey back in time with early advertising, packaging and retailing artefacts, postage stamps, commemorative china and dividend tokens.

i 31 Toad Lane, Rochdale

T (01706) 524 920
http://museum.co-op.ac.uk

Rochdale Town Hall (free)

Completed in 1871 at a cost of £155,000, Rochdale Town Hall is widely regarded as one of the finest Victorian town halls in Britain. The Grand Staircase, the magnificent Great Hall, fresco, stained glass, statuary, ceramics and paintings all add to the grandeur of an exuberant expression of civic pride.

i The Esplanade, Rochdale

T (01706) 864 797
www.rochdale.gov.uk

❀ Phone for opening times

working 18th-century water-powered cotton mill

Salford Museum & Art Gallery (free)

Features an authentic period street from 1890, complete with shops and houses. New to the museum is the Lifetimes Gallery, which showcases Salford's past and present. Meanwhile, the Victorian Gallery features sculptures, paintings, pottery, furniture and decorative arts. See also p.30.

ℹ Peel Park, The Crescent, Salford

T (0161) 778 0800
www.salford.gov.uk/
salfordmuseum

✵ Mon-Fri 10-4.45, Sat-Sun 1-5

Setantii (free)

This atmospheric visitor attraction traces the history of Tameside from Celtic times to the present day. Families will love the olden day figures, replica armour and the Anderson air raid shelter with its wartime sound effects.

ℹ Town Hall Building,
Ashton-under-Lyne

T (0161) 342 2812
www.tameside.gov.uk/
museumsandgalleries

✵ Mon-Fri 10-4, Sat 10-1

Staircase House (£)

This exciting new attraction invites you to time travel through the history of Staircase House from 1460 to World War II. You are invited to smell, touch and listen, and to relive its history by pulling back the bedclothes on the four-poster bed, peeling rush lights, and trying your hand at 17th-century quill pen writing.

ℹ 30-31 Market Place, Stockport

T (0161) 480 1460
www.staircasehouse.org.uk

✵ Mon-Sat 12-5, Sun 1-5

Stockport Museum (free)

Set in a beautiful location with outstanding views, this historic building retains many of its original features and provides historical information about Stockport. One of the first purpose-built museums in the country.

ℹ Vernon Park, Turncroft Lane,
Offerton, Stockport

T (0161) 474 4460
www.stockport.gov.uk/
heritageattractions

✵ Mon-Fri 10-4, Sat-Sun 11-5

Wythenshawe Hall (£)

A splendid timber-framed house dating from Tudor times, set in the beautiful grounds of Wythenshawe Park. Original features from the 1540 building can be seen alongside later additions in the centuries following.

ℹ Wythenshawe Park, Northenden

T (0161) 998 2331
www.manchester.gov.uk

✵ Phone for opening times

time travel
through
history

Art Galleries and Exhibitions

Admission prices for the following galleries are graded according to the price of a single adult admission:
£ = under £5; ££ = £5-£10; £££ = over £10

⭐ Central Manchester

ArTzu (free)
There is a definite buzz about ArTzu Gallery which is situated in the Northern Quarter and boasts a wide range of vibrant canvases and artistic styles. Big names jostle with artistic newcomers and the varying styles demonstrate the breadth of the collection in this open and attractive venue.

- 🛈 Virginia House, 5 Great Ancoats St
- **T** (0161) 228 3001
  www.artzu.co.uk
- ✺ Tues-Sat 11-5.30

Castlefield Gallery (free/£)
A contemporary art gallery with a changing programme of exhibitions and educational events. Other features include The Portfolio Space (featuring artwork by North West artists) and the Greater Manchester studio group database.

- 🛈 2 Hewitt Street, Knott Mill
- **T** (0161) 832 8034
  www.castlefieldgallery.co.uk
- ✺ Wed-Sun 1-6

Chinese Arts Centre (free/£)
The Chinese Arts Centre offers changing contemporary arts exhibitions, workshops, education programmes and information.
See also p.8.

- 🛈 Thomas Street
- **T** (0161) 832 7271
  www.chinese-arts-centre.org
- ✺ Opening times vary; please phone

Cornerhouse (free)
Manchester's lively centre for international cinema and visual arts. Its three galleries exhibit contemporary art, sculpture and photography, while three cinema screens show a wide variety of independent films. See also p.9.

- 🛈 70 Oxford Road
- **T** (0161) 200 1500
  www.cornerhouse.org
- ✺ Daily 11-11

CUBE Gallery (free/£)
CUBE is one of Europe's most exciting architecture and design centres, dedicated to broadcasting the ideas and issues that lie behind buildings and spaces that make up our built environment. Consisting of three gallery spaces and seminar rooms, the centre is a unique hub for art and design in the North West.

- 🛈 113-115 Portland Street
- **T** (0161) 237 5525
  www.cube.org.uk
- ✺ Opening times vary; please phone

vibrant
canvases
and artistic
styles

Art Galleries and Exhibitions

Gallery of Costume (free)
Delve into the Gallery of Costume's collection of 20,000 items of clothing. See also p.10.

- Platt Hall, Wilmslow Road
- **T** (0161) 224 5217
  http://www.manchester galleries.org
- ✹ Last Sat of month 10-5, or by appointment

Imperial War Museum North (free)
Hosts a regular series of themed art exhibitions exploring how people's lives are shaped by war and conflict. See also p.12.

- *i* The Quays, Trafford Wharf Road
- **T** (0161) 836 4000
  www.iwm.org.uk/north
- ✹ Daily 10-6

Manchester Art Gallery (free)
The revamped Manchester Art Gallery houses one of the world's finest collections of art, displayed in spectacular surroundings. There are also fun interactive exhibits and special exhibitions to enjoy. See also p.15.

- *i* Mosley Street
- **T** (0161) 235 8888
  www.manchestergalleries.org
- ✹ Tues-Sun 10-5

Manchester Craft & Design Centre (free)
A spacious, flood-lit oasis in Manchester's Northern Quarter, packed with original pieces of art, craft and design – all of it for sale. The centre comprises 18 studios and hosts an ongoing programme of unusual exhibitions. See also p.19.

- *i* 17 Oak Street
- **T** (0161) 832 4274
  www.craftanddesign.com
- ✹ Mon-Sat 10-5.30

Manchester Town Hall (free)
This magnificent building is home to many treasures, including the Ford Maddox Brown murals, which are monument to the ideas of Victorian Manchester. See also p.22.

- *i* Albert Square
- **T** (0161) 234 5000
  www.manchester.gov.uk
- ✹ Mon-Fri 9-5

The Portico Library and Gallery (free)
A beautifully restored Georgian, private-subcription library, founded in 1806 and renowned from Victorian days. The gallery, which is open to the public during weekdays, hosts a range of exhibitions.

- *i* 57 Mosley Street
- **T** (0161) 236 6785
  www.theportico.org.uk
- ✹ Mon-Fri 9.30-4.30

Urbis (free)
Located in the heart of Manchester, Urbis is an exhibition centre dedicated to city life, featuring interactive exhibits and dynamic changing exhibitions which explore the people, place and pulse of the modern city. See also p.34.

- *i* Cathedral Gardens
- **T** (0161) 605 8200
  www.urbis.org.uk
- ✹ Tues-Sun 10-6

Whitworth Art Gallery (free)
The Gallery is home to a famous collection of British watercolours, modern and historic prints, drawings, paintings and sculptures, textiles and wallpapers. See also p.35.

- *i* University of Manchester, Oxford Road

beautifully restored Georgian library

T (0161) 275 7450
www.whitworth.man.ac.uk
❀ Mon-Sat 10-5, Sun 2-5

Waterside Arts Centre (free/£)

Sale Waterside is a vibrant new venue at the heart of Trafford in a stunning waterside location. There are a variety of flexible arts and events spaces including a 350-seat theatre, exhibition gallery, creative learning spaces and a unique outdoor events plaza with bars and restaurants.

i 1 Waterside Plaza, Sale Waterside
T (0161) 912 5616
www.watersideartscentre.co.uk
❀ Mon-Sat 10-5.30

❋ Greater Manchester

The Astley Cheetham Art Gallery (free)

Astley Cheetham Art Gallery is a small, one-room gallery which shows a variety of temporary exhibitions of various art forms, including photography and local history. The gallery also holds what is said to be one of the best small painting collections in the country.

i Trinity Street, Stalybridge
T (0161) 338 2708
www.tameside.gov.uk/
museumsandgalleries
❀ Mon-Wed and Fri 10-12.30 and
1-5, Sat 9-12.30 and 1-4

Bankley Studios Gallery (free/£)

The studio currently has over 30 artists in residence working across a range of disciplines including painting, textiles, photography, installation, sculpture and ceramics. In addition to the studio spaces there is also an artist-run gallery space.

i Bankley Street, Levenshulme
T (0161) 256 4143
www.bankley.org.uk
❀ Opening times vary; please phone

Bolton Museum, Art Gallery and Aquarium (free)

A family-friendly museum with a wildlife gallery and activity centre, Egyptian mummies, an aquarium and art gallery. Lays on an an innovative programme of changing exhibitions.

i Le Mans Crescent, Bolton
T (01204) 332 211
www.boltonmuseums.org.uk
❀ Mon-Sat 9-5

Borland Gallery (free)

A new gallery space located within the University of Salford. Presenting a dynamic and experimental programme of exhibitions and events, the Borland Gallery showcases work by staff, students, graduates and resident artists at the University. The space aims to embrace risk, rigour and diversity.

i University of Salford
T (0161) 295 5223
www.salford.ac.uk
❀ Opening times vary; please phone

Bureau Gallery (free)

A new, purpose-built, independent art gallery providing a platform for dynamic, exciting and experimental work by emerging and established national and international artists. In addition to exhibitions, Bureau presents live events such as artists' film and video screenings and experimental music.

i Islington Mill, James Street, Salford
T 07757 956 555
www.bureaugallery.com
❀ Wed-Sat 11-5

vibrant new
venue at
the heart of
Trafford

Bury Art Gallery, Museum & Archive (free)

Home to the Wrigley collection of Victorian art and cutting-edge temporary exhibitions. This is also the location of the new Museum & Archive Centre, which traces Bury's history through changing displays and local records.

T (0161) 253 5878
www.bury.gov.uk

❋ Tues-Fri 10-5, Sat 10-4.30

Central Art Gallery (free)

Located above the library, these beautiful gallery spaces host a varied programme of temporary exhibitions. There is something to suit everyone's taste with group and solo shows of artists from the region including paintings, sculpture, installation and textiles.

ℹ Central Library Building, Old Street, Ashton-under-Lyne

T (0161) 342 2650
www.tameside.gov.uk/museumsandgalleries

❋ Tues, Wed and Fri 10-12.30 and 1-5, Thurs 1-7.30, Sat 9-12.30 and 1-4

Drumcroon Gallery (free/££)

Ongoing exhibitions by contemporary artists aimed at offering young people, their teachers and the local community access to the range, breadth and variety of the visual arts. The centre provides its visitors with opportunities to engage in related practical activities.

ℹ Parsons Walk, Wigan

T (01942) 321 840
www.drumcroon.org.uk

❋ Opening times vary; please phone

Gallery Oldham (free)

Lively contemporary gallery showing paintings, crafts and photography from local, national and international artists. Gallery Oldham offers a range of activities throughout the year, including a percussion and dance workshop on Monday evenings for all the family and Saturday live music events.

ℹ Oldham Cultural Quarter, Greaves Street, Oldham

T (0161) 911 4653
www.galleryoldham.org.uk

❋ Mon-Sat 10-5

Havana Arts Gallery and Studio (free)

An exotic collection of Cuban art, all of it for sale. The gallery is the sole supplier of Cuban art in Britain. Most of the works of art are displayed on the website, along with details about the artists involved.

ℹ 24 Kay Street, Rawtenstall

T (01706) 228882
www.havana-arts.co.uk

❋ Please phone ahead for opening times

The ImiTate© Gallery (£/££)

ImiTate© Gallery is a unique public art venue that will showcase the work of artists near and far, from Manchester and beyond. Call by regularly, and you will witness an ever-changing display of artwork that will beguile and inspire even the most jaded of visitors.

ℹ 623 Stockport Road, Longsight

T (0161) 225 1200
www.imitate.org.uk

❋ Please phone ahead for opening times

Irwell Sculpture Trail (free)

The largest public arts scheme in the North West. There are currently 30 sculptures by regional, national and international artists which celebrate the area's heritage and landscape. The

sole supplier of Cuban art

Art Galleries and Exhibitions

works have been developed in clusters along a 30-mile footpath from Salford Quays.

ℹ Bury Tourist Information Centre
☎ (0161) 253 5111
www.irwellsculpturetrail.co.uk
❋ Permanently open

Littleborough Coach House & Heritage Centre (free)

This historic coach house from the late 18th century hosts regular exhibitions by local artists. See also p.39.

ℹ Lodge Street, Littleborough, Rochdale
☎ (01706) 378 481
❋ Tues-Fri and Sun 1.30-4, Sat 11-4

The Lowry (free)

A stunning landmark, The Lowry captures that unusual combination of functionality and beauty, as stainless steel and glass merge with water and light. See also p.32.

ℹ The Lowry, Pier 8, Salford Quays
☎ 0870 787 5780
www.thelowry.com
❋ Tue-Sat 10-8, Sun-Mon 10-6

Saddleworth Museum and Art Gallery (£)

Housed in a former textile mill, the museum gallery features work by contemporary artists alongside travelling exhibitions. The museum itself features local archaeology, handicrafts and items of textile machinery.

ℹ High Street, Uppermill, Oldham
☎ (01457) 874 093
www.saddleworthmuseum.co.uk
❋ Summer Mon-Sat 10-4.30, Sun 12-4; winter Mon-Sun 1-4

Salford Museum & Art Gallery (free)

New to the museum is the Lifetimes Gallery, which showcases Salford's past and present. Meanwhile, the Victorian Gallery features sculptures, paintings, pottery, furniture and decorative arts. See also p.30.

ℹ Peel Park, The Crescent, Salford
☎ (0161) 778 0800
www.salford.gov.uk/salfordmuseum
❋ Mon-Fri 10-4.45, Sat-Sun 1-5

Stockport Art Gallery (free)

A magnificent Greco-Roman art gallery and war memorial in the heart of Stockport. An ever-changing contemporary exhibition programme of local, national and international significance. Selected displays from Stockport, with permanent collections of 19th- and 20th-century paintings and sculptures.

ℹ Wellington Road South, Stockport
☎ (0161) 474 4453
www.stockport.gov.uk
❋ Mon-Tues and Thurs-Fri 11-5, Sat 10-5

Turnpike Gallery (free/££)

The Turnpike Gallery specialises in temporary exhibitions by regional, national and international artists reflecting the broad variety of current arts practice. Each exhibition is accompanied by educational events. The gallery also accommodates an artist in residence – visitors welcome.

ℹ Civic Square, Leigh
☎ (01942) 404 469
www.wlct.org
❋ Mon-Fri 10-6, Sat 9.30-3.30

magnificent Greco-Roman art

Admission prices for the following venues are graded according to the price of a single adult admission:
£ = under £10; ££ = £10-£20; £££ = over £20

⚑ Classical & Opera

Bridgewater Hall (£££)

This state-of-the-art 2,400 seat auditorium, with magnificent Marcussen pipe organ, opened in September 1996. Concerts range from classical and jazz through to world and popular music. It is the home of Manchester's renowned Hallé Orchestra as well as being the performance base for the city's other distinguished ensembles, the BBC Philharmonic and Manchester Camerata.

- *i* Lower Mosley Street, Manchester M2 3WS
- **T** (0161) 907 9000
  www.bridgewater-hall.co.uk
- ❀ Mon-Sat 10-6, Sun 12-6 (later for concerts)
- + *Café, restaurant, internet access, disabled access*

Manchester Evening News Arena (£££)

The MEN Arena is Europe's largest and most impressive indoor concert venue, receiving a staggering 1.2 million customers every year. Voted International Venue of the Year 2002 and officially the Busiest Concert Venue in the World in 2004, the MEN Arena hosts a wide range of entertainment from rock, pop and classical music concerts to family shows and world-class sporting events.

The MEN Arena is situated at Victoria railway station. For the Box Office, call 0870 190 8000.

- *i* Hunt's Bank, Manchester M3 1AR
- **T** 0871 226 5000
  www.men-arena.com
- ❀ Open for performances
- + *Café, disabled access*

Royal Northern College of Music (free/£)

Two auditoria make this a major musical venue for classical music, jazz and opera performed by top international professionals as well as the RNCM's acclaimed student ensembles. Occasional art and sculpture exhibitions are hosted here too, sometimes with musical connections.

- *i* 124 Oxford Road, Manchester M13 9RD
- **T** (0161) 907 5555
  www.rncm.ac.uk
- ❀ Open for concerts, also Open Days
- + *Café, disabled access*

the renowned Hallé Orchestra

Opera House (££/£££)

A touring theatre venue hosting large West End musicals, drama, children's shows and concerts (jazz, classical and pop). The Opera House opened as the 'New Theatre' in 1912, but was renamed the Opera House in recognition of the success of Sir Thomas Beecham, who brought his operas to the theatre.

- *i* Opera House, Quay Street, Manchester, M3 3HP
- **T** 0870 060 1826
  www.manchestertheatres.co.uk
- ☀ Open for performances
- + *Bar, disabled access*

Palace Theatre (££/£££)

The Palace Theatre first opened in 1891 and went on to host some of the great acts from the Music Hall era, including Charlie Chaplin and Lillie Langtry. Today, the busy venue plays home to a range of entertainment, from classical music to musicals and drama.

- *i* Palace Theatre, Oxford Street, Manchester, M1 6FT
- **T** 0870 060 1826
  www.manchestertheatres.co.uk
- ☀ Open for performances
- + *Bar, disabled access*

🎵 Jazz & Blues

Matt & Phred's Jazz Club (free/£)

Matt & Phred's is the only club in the North dedicated to live jazz. Many people rate it as their favourite bar in Manchester. There's a relaxed atmosphere and top quality live jazz almost every night served up along with fine food and drink, from pizzas to tapas. There's an extensive wine list too.

- *i* 64 Tib Street, Manchester, M4 1LW
- **T** (0161) 831 7002
  www.mattandphreds.com
- ☀ Mon-Sat 5pm-2am
- + *Restaurant, bar*

Opera House (££/£££)

See above, under 'Classical & Opera'.

- *i* Opera House, Quay Street, Manchester, M3 3HP
- **T** 0870 060 1826
  www.manchestertheatres.co.uk
- ☀ Open for performances
- + *Bar, disabled access*

Royal Northern College of Music (free/£)

See above, under 'Classical & Opera'.

- *i* 124 Oxford Road, Manchester M13 9RD
- **T** (0161) 907 5555
  www.rncm.ac.uk
- ☀ Open for concerts, also Open Days
- + *Café, disabled access*

The Green Room (£)

Hosts occasional jazz and blues gigs, and serves as an intimate venue for the annual Manchester Jazz Festival (held in July). See also 'Theatre & Performance' below.

- *i* 54-56 Whitworth Street, Manchester M1 5WW
- **T** (0161) 615 0500
  www.greenroomarts.org
- ☀ Wed-Sat 5-late
- + *Café-bar, disabled access*

annual Manchester Jazz Festival

Music, Theatre and the Performing Arts

🎵 Pop, Rock & Indie

Manchester Academy (£/££)

A Student Union venue specialising in new, up-and-coming and unsigned bands. The Academy also hosts big-name pop and rock acts every now and then.

- 🗐 Oxford Road,
  Manchester M13 9PR
- (0161) 275 2930
  www.manchesteracademy.net
- ✳ Open for performances
- *Bar, disabled access*

Manchester Apollo (££/£££)

One of Manchester's longest-standing concert venues, second only in size to the Manchester Evening News Arena (below). Virtually all of the top names in pop and rock music have performed here at one time or another. The concert hall has two levels – the upper level has seating and the lower level is usually standing-only.

- 🗐 Stockport Road, Ardwick Green
  Manchester M12
- (0161) 242 2560.
  www.alive.co.uk/apollo
- ✳ Open for performances
  Bar, disabled access

Manchester Evening News (MEN) Arena (££/£££)

This enormous arena plays host to major mainstream pop acts. See also under 'Classical & Opera' above.

- 🗐 Hunt's Bank,
  Manchester M3 1AR
- 0871 226 5000
  www.men-arena.com
- ✳ Open for performances
  Bar, disabled access

Night & Day Café (£)

Manchester's top Rock 'n' Roll Bar, with live music every day of the week. Serves good food, too, and the Long Bar is open daily until 2am.

- *i* 26 Oldham Street,
  Manchester M1 1JN
- **T** (0161) 236 1822
  www.nightnday.org
- 🎵 Open daily 10am-2am
- **+** *Bar, restaurant, disabled access*

The Roadhouse (£)

The Roadhouse has long been a key stop on any up-and-coming band's tour. Not the most glamorous of venues, but its history speaks for itself, with the likes of Oasis, the Verve, Coldplay and Chemical Brothers all cutting their teeth here.

- *i* 8 Newton Street, Piccadilly,
  Manchester M1 2AN
- **T** (0161) 237 9789
  www.theroadhouselive.co.uk
- 🎵 Opening times vary,
  often 8pm-2am
- **+** *Bar*

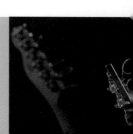

top names
in pop and
rock music

❇ Theatre & Performance

Contact Theatre (free/£)

A space for drama, dance, spoken word and urban art. The Contact Theatre also has workshops and courses for both adults and young people. The Sola Café Bar is open until late at weekends.

- *i* Devas Street,
  Manchester M15 6JA
- **T** (0161) 274 0600
  www.contact-theatre.org
- ✸ Daily 10am-11pm
- + *Café, restaurant, disabled access*

Library Theatre Company (££)

An intimate 312-seat space in the basement of Central Library, with an enviable reputation for its challenging productions of the work of American playwrights such as David Mamet, Arthur Miller and Tennessee Williams, as well as plays not previously seen in the North West – notably the work of David Hare and Alan Ayckbourn. At least one performance of each in-house production is audio-described, British Sign Language interpreted, and captioned.

- *i* Central Library, St Peter's Square,
  Manchester M2 5PD
- **T** (0161) 236 7110
  www.librarytheatre.com
- ✸ Open for performances
- + *Café, restaurant, disabled access*

The Green Room (£)

The Green Room is a space for presenting and creating new and innovative performances. It offers a varied programme of theatre, dance, live art and music from the best of the international, national and local arts scene. Fully licensed bar, meeting room and performing spaces are all available for private hire. See also 'Jazz & Blues' above.

- *i* 54-56 Whitworth Street,
  Manchester M1 5WW
- **T** (0161) 615 0500
  www.greenroomarts.org
- ✸ Wed-Sat 5-late
- + *Café-bar, disabled access*

Royal Exchange Theatre (£/£££)

As well as hosting a varied programme of plays and other special events, the theatre also houses a bookshop, craft centre and foyer gallery, which is recognised as a major focal point of contemporary craft work in the North West. The coffee bar and brasserie offer an alternative to the bustle of the city.

- *i* St Ann's Square,
  Manchester M2 7DH
- **T** (0161) 833 9833
  www.royalexchange.co.uk
- ✸ Open for performances
- + *Bookshop, craft centre, café, restaurant, disabled access*

54
Eating and Drinking

Prices for the following eateries are graded according to the average cost of a main course:
£ = under £10; ££ = £10-£15; £££ = over £15

🔲 British Restaurants

Brasserie on Portland (££)
A popular brasserie situated on the ground floor of the Princess Hotel – a converted silk warehouse from Victorian times, now upmarket and stylish. The restaurant has a sophisticated ambience in bright modern surroundings.

i Best Western Princess Hotel, Portland Street M1 6DF

T (0161) 236 5122
www.princessonportland.co.uk
& Good

The B Lounge (£)
A stylish and popular gastro-pub, previously known as The Bridge, and serving a range of traditional British dishes – all in healthy servings.

i 58 Bridge Street, Manchester M3 3BW

T (0161) 834 0242
www.theblounge.co.uk
& Good

Choice Bar & Restaurant (£££)
An award-winning Modern British restaurant and bar featuring live piano music and Manchester's largest collection of wine by the glass. Awarded two AA rosettes.

i Castle Quay, Castlefield, Manchester, M15 4NT

T (0161) 833 3400
www.choicebarandrestaurant.co.uk
& Good

Lass O'Gowrie Brewhouse (£)
One of the city's most famous traditional pubs, the Lass provides nine real ales and fine traditional food every day. The welcome is legendary, and the guest ale spot on.

i 36 Charles Street, Manchester M1 7DB

T (0161) 273 6932
www.thelass.co.uk
& Good

Love Saves The Day (££)
An award-winning deli, café and wine merchant. Retailing and serving great quality, independently sourced food and drink in an informal atmosphere.

i 345 Deansgate, Manchester M3 4LG

T (0161) 834 2266
www.lovesavestheday.com

cutting-edge Modern British cuisine

Mr Thomas's Chophouse (££)
A genuine Victorian bar, restaurant and coffee shop built more than a century ago. Serves fine wine, beer and excellent traditional British food.

i 52 Cross Street,
Manchester, M2 7AR
T (0161) 832 2245
www.tomschophouse.com

Manchester 235 (££)
The first luxury dining, gaming and live music club in the UK. The club is influenced by the newly-hip Las Vegas scene, boasting contemporary interiors, gaming, bar facilities and two distinct restaurants – Italian 'Numero' and Modern British 'Linen'.

i Watson Street,
Manchester M3 4LP
T (0161) 832 3927
www.manchester235.co.uk

Market Restaurant (££)
The original Northern Quarter restaurant serving top quality seasonal food in a relaxed atmosphere. The wine list is carefully chosen and moderately priced, while the speciality beer list is exceptional.

i 104 High Street Quarter,
Manchester M4 1HQ
T (0161) 834 3743
www.market-restaurant.com
& Good

Sam's Chophouse (££)
This atmospheric tile-and-timber restaurant serves classic British cuisine, with delightful seasonal dishes made to order. The wine list is as good as any in the region and there is even an in-house ale.

i Back Pool Fold, Chapel Walks,
Manchester M2 1HN
T (0161) 834 3210
www.samschophouse.com

Simply Heathcotes (£££)
Specialises in great British dishes using the best locally sourced ingredients, from Fell-bred lamb and Whitby cod to local asparagus and raspberries.

i Jacksons Row,
Manchester M2 5WD
T (0161) 835 3536
www.heathcotes.co.uk
& Good

Waxy O'Connors (£)
A warren of staircases and passages links nine separate zones, with three bars and a busy restaurant serving a wide-ranging menu. Cathedral-like timber carvings and beautiful tiled floors make for a unique atmosphere.

i The Printworks Corporation Street,
Manchester M4 2BS
T (0161) 835 1210
www.waxyoconnors.co.uk/
manchester
& Good

the best
locally
sourced
ingredients

⭐ European Restaurants

Croma (£)

An independent gourmet pizzeria in Central Manchester, offering a selection of traditional and gourmet pizzas, together with Mediterranean salads and oven-baked pasta. Croma is a multi-level, light and airy restaurant, and combines great style with value.

- *i* 1 Clarence Street, Manchester M2 4DE
- **T** (0161) 237 9799
  www.cromamanchester.co.uk
- ♿ Good

Dukes 92 (£)

A favourite canalside watering hole with a full menu ranging from sandwiches and snacks to constantly changing pasta dishes and chef's specials. Dukes is known for its speciality cheese counter, which offers almost 50 cheeses and patés from around Europe.

- *i* 18 Castle Street, Castlefield, Manchester M3 4LZ
- **T** (0161) 839 8656
  www.dukes92.com
- ♿ Good

Evuna (££)

Evuna offers a taste of real Spain, with everything from a light tapas lunch to a full traditional Spanish meal. Evuna is also a specialist importer of fine Spanish wines, many of which are not available elsewhere in the UK.

- *i* 277 Deansgate, Manchester M3 4EW
- **T** (0161) 819 8752
  www.evuna.com

Le Mont (£££)

Manchester's first elevated restaurant, superbly located within the Millennium Quarter, on the 5th and 6th levels of Urbis. Offers exquisite Modern French cuisine with unique views over Manchester's urban landscape.

- *i* Urbis, Cathedral Gardens, Manchester M4 3BG
- **T** (0161) 605 8282
  www.urbis.org.uk/lemont
- ♿ Good

Le Petit Blanc (££)

With Raymond Blanc at the helm, Le Petit Blanc combines original French cuisine with a modern vision. A wide range of light and wholesome dishes are served, and the atmosphere is surprisingly relaxed and non-snooty.

- *i* 55 King Street, Manchester M2 4LQ
- **T** (0161) 832 1000
  www.lepetitblanc.co.uk
- ♿ Good

The Living Room (££)

A neighbourhood-based restaurant and bar serving good, honest, robust and stylish food with its origins firmly in the European tradition.

- *i* 80 Deansgate, Manchester M3 2ER
- **T** (0161) 832 0083
  www.thelivingroom.co.uk
- ♿ Good

speciality cheese counter

58
Eating and Drinking

Obsidian Bar & Restaurant (£££)

The menu here pays tribute to Obsidian's North West roots by making use of the finest local produce. Hearty food, beautifully cooked and served in very stylish surroundings.

i Arora International Hotel,
18-24 Princess Street,
Manchester M1 4LY

T (0161) 236 4348
www.obsidianmanchester.co.uk

Olive Press (££)

Popular Italian dishes using the freshest ingredients. Dishes are served straight from the char grill and brick-fired oven, while the handmade pastas and stone-baked pizzas make this an Italian experience with a difference.

i 4 Lloyd Street, off Deansgate,
Manchester M2 5AB

T (0161) 832 9090
www.olivepresspizzeria.co.uk

& Good

Stock Restaurant (££)

Classic Italian cuisine, from antipasti and homemade gnocchi to the legendary Steak Fiorentina and Mixed Seafood Platter – all served within the Edwardian splendour of Manchester's former Stock Exchange.

i 4 Norfolk Street,
Manchester M2 1DW

T (0161) 839 6644
www.stockrestaurant.co.uk

& Good

Asian Restaurants

Ikan Thai & Oriental Restaurant (£)

A hidden gem in Sackville Street, serving all the usual Thai favourites and using the freshest ingredients. The tables are set around a bath full of carp.

i 68 Sackville Street,
Manchester, M1 3NJ

T (0161) 236 1313

Little Yang Sing (££)

Quality Cantonese cuisine served in a refined atmosphere, with excellent dim sum and a big range of vegetarian dishes.

i 17 George Street,
Manchester M1 4HE

T (0161) 228 7722
www.littleyangsing.co.uk

Lotus (£)

Set over three levels and decorated with 'oriental chic' in mind. The cuisine is a contemporary fusion of East meets West, while a spectacular roof garden has opened recently.

i 35a King Street,
Manchester M2 6AA

T (0161) 832 9724
www.lotusbyyangsing.com

New Samsi (£)

An atmospheric Japanese restaurant with sunken tables and a vast menu of Japanese dishes, from sushi and sashimi to tempura and teriyaki – all at good prices.

i 36 Whitworth Street,
Manchester M1 3NR

T (0161) 279 0022

oriental
chic

Eating and Drinking

Pan Asia (£)
Pan Asia serves a panoply of Southeast Asian cuisine, from Chinese, Japanese and Thai to Malaysian and Vietnamese.

- *i* 45-47 Faulkner Street, Manchester M1 4HE
- **T** (0161) 236 6868
  www.pan-asia.co.uk
- & Good

Pearl City (£)
Serves a wide variety of traditional Chinese cuisine, with specialities ranging across the Provinces. Offers a good range of imitation meat dishes using soya bean products.

- *i* 33 George Street, Manchester M1 4HF
- **T** (0161) 228 7683

Siam Orchid (£)
One of the UK's first Thai restaurants to open outside London (back in 1985), this place still lives up to its reputation for tasty Thai cuisine at great prices.

- *i* 54 Portland Street, Manchester M1 4QU
- **T** (0161) 236 1388
- & Good

Wings Restaurant (£)
An award-winning Chinese restaurant serving contemporary Cantonese cuisine, with more than 150 dishes to choose from. Occupies the smart city-centre site that was once The Lincoln.

- *i* 1 Lincoln Square, Manchester M2 5LN
- **T** (0161) 834 9000
  www.wingsrestaurant.co.uk

Yang Sing (££)
One of Europe's leading Cantonese restaurants. From a tasty Dim Sum lunch to a conference dinner, the Yang Sing provides exceptional value.

- *i* 34 Princess Street, Manchester M1 4JY
- **T** (0161) 236 2200
  www.yang-sing.com

Global/American Restaurants

Cocoa Rooms (£££)
Situated within six vaulted arches, with a simple yet sophisticated menu that will take you on a gastronomic tour of the globe. There's an extensive wine and cocktail list, and outdoor dining with views of the river.

- *i* 1-6 Chapel Street, Manchester M3 7NJ
- **T** 07921 439 480
  www.thecocoarooms.com

Grinch Wine Bar (££)
Something of an institution in Manchester, with its unique decor, friendly service and tasty, uncomplicated food. Perfect for lunching, meeting, chatting…

- *i* 5-7 Chapel Walks, Manchester M2 1HN
- **T** (0161) 907 3210
  www.grinch.co.uk

曼彻斯特中国城
CHINA TOWN MANCHESTER

gastronomic tour of the globe

Eating and Drinking

Hard Rock Café (££)
The UK's largest Hard Rock Café, with authentic American fare, generous drinks and an awe-inspiring collection of rock memorabilia.

- *i* The Printworks, Manchester M4 2BS
- **T** (0161) 831 6700
- www.hardrock.com
- & Good

Loaf (££)
An ultra-modern, stylish bar-restaurant with a nightclub in the basement. Set in the Deansgate Locks Development, this venue spans two floors and is set in two huge railway arches.

- *i* Deansgate Locks Arches 3a and 5, Whitworth Street West, Manchester M1 5LH
- **T** (0161) 819 5858
- www.loaf-manchester.co.uk
- & Good

Opus (££)
Opus offers a variety of experiences: private dining or a table at Ink Brasserie, dancing in one of two club rooms, laughing at the very best in live stand-up comedy, or enjoying great live bands.

- *i* The Printworks, Withy Grove, Manchester M4 2BS
- **T** (0161) 834 2414
- www.opusmanchester.com
- & Good

Panacea Bar & Restaurant (££)
A bar and restaurant with a refreshing, light atmosphere and professional service; a favourite for business lunches and after-work drinks.

- *i* 14 John Dalton Street, Manchester M2 6JR
- **T** (0161) 833 0000
- www.panaceamanchester.co.uk
- & Good

Room (££)
A unique mix of antique and retro makes this a stunning place to enjoy dining experience. There is a separat cocktail lounge, too, and a private dining room.

- *i* 81 King Street, Spring Gardens, Manchester M2 4ST
- **T** (0161) 839 2005
- www.roomrestaurants.com
- & Good

Taurus (£)
A haven of sanity and sophistication Canal Street, in the heart of Manchester's Gay Village. Offers wines, cocktails, champagne and a wide selection of hot and cold food including huge platters to share.

- *i* 1 Canal Street, Manchester M1 3HE
- **T** (0161) 236 4593
- www.taurus-bar.co.uk
- & Good

Tiger Tiger (££)
Manchester's premier venue for the over-25s, offering six bars, a restaura and a club over four floors. Each bar has its own style and ambience, while the restaurant offers customers the flexibility to grab a quick bite with friends or take time to enjoy a full-on dining experience.

- *i* The Printworks, Withy Grove, Manchester M4 2BS
- **T** (0161) 385 8080
- www.tigertiger-manch.co.uk
- & Good

set in two huge railway arches

Eating and Drinking

Bars

See also: Choice Bar & Restaurant, Cocoa Rooms, Crisp Bar & Restaurant, Dukes 92, Grinch Wine Bar, The Living Room, Loaf, Manchester 235, Obsidian Bar & Restaurant, Opus, Panacea Bar & Restaurant, Room, Taurus, Tiger Tiger, Waxy O'Connors – all listed above under 'Restaurants'.

Ampersand
Probably the most glamorous bar and club in Manchester, with a stunning, richly decorated interior and a sound-system to match.

i Longworth Street,
Manchester M3 4BQ

T (0161) 832 3038
www.theampersand.co.uk

The Britons Protection
One of Manchester's oldest pubs, with more than 150 different varieties of whisky and a beer garden.

i 50 Great Bridgewater Street,
Manchester M1 5LE

T (0161) 236 5895

Beluga
A friendly and warm atmosphere with stylish and chic clientele. The basement houses an exceptional restaurant serving an opulent a la carte menu, complimented by one of the city's most extensive selections of fine wines, champagne and cocktails.

i Mount Street,
Manchester M2 5WQ

T (0161) 833 3339
www.belugaonline.co.uk

Gaia
A grand, former cotton warehouse, with a plush interior of all-leather seats and dark-wood tables. A laid-back bar attracting a mixed, mellow crowd.

i 46 Sackville Street,
Manchester M1 3WF

T (0161) 228 1002

One Central Street
Described as 'the most stylish bar in Manchester' by Elle magazine, One Central Street offers great service, great music and an extensive drinks menu in chic, contemporary surroundings.

i 1 Central Street,
Manchester M2 5WR

T 0870 740 4000
www.onecentralstreet.co.uk

Paparazzi
A tardis-style entrance leads down to a spacious bar with split-level dance floors. Good cocktail list.

i The Printworks,
Manchester M4 2BS

T (0161) 832 1234
www.thepaparazzi.co.uk

Sports Café
The Sports Café has a capacity of 1,750 and features five separate bars, a dance floor and two dining areas. The café screens all international sport and archive footage.

i 23 Quay Street,
Manchester M3 4AE

T (0161) 839 8800
www.thesportscafe.com

Sugar Lounge
A hot addition to the Manchester bar scene, with knowledgeable bar staff who know how to mix a fine cocktail. Funky decor to go with the funky music.

i Deansgate Locks,
Manchester M1 5LH

T (0161) 834 6500
www.sugarloungebar.com

chic,
contemporary
surroundings

✣ Shopping Centres

Afflecks Palace

An emporium of cutting-edge fashion, music memorabilia and bizarre alternative art. Afflecks Palace does its best to nurture interesting independent boutiques and fledgling entrepreneurs, standing by its ethic to provide a challenge to those larger shopping centres based entirely on commercial interests.

Shops housed within Afflecks Palace include Moonwalk Collectables (specialises in Star Wars and Dr Who collectables), Attic Fancy Dress (prize-winning theme and retro costumes for hire and sale), Vampire Bunnies (unique handmade and customised clothing for guys and girls), and Extreme Largeness (probably the largest selection of jewellery and accessories in Manchester).

i 52 Church Street,
   Manchester M4 1PW

T (0161) 834 2039
   www.afflecks-palace.co.uk
Facilities: accessible with assistance, major credit cards accepted, passenger lift, toilets on premises, parking nearby.

❋ Opening hours: Mon-Fri 10.30-6, Sat 10-6

Harvey Nichols

Fashionistas everywhere can breathe a sigh of relief; Harvey Nichols Manchester has brought a unique and accessible shopping experience to those living in the North West. The ground floor hosts a series of accessory and jewellery boutiques from designers and niche brands.

The food market specialises in a delectable selection of Harvey Nichols' own products, in addition to large selection of food and drink from around the world. The beauty arena provides the very best in skincare, colour and fragrance with many brands exclusive to Harvey Nichols. Both Women's and Menswear offer excellent contemporary and casualwear in addition to an elegant shoe department.

i 21 New Cathedral Street,
   Manchester M1 1AD

T (0161) 828 8888
   www.harveynichols.co.uk
Facilities: café, brasserie, bar, restaurant, accessible with assistance, major credit cards taken, passenger lift, toilets on premises, parking nearby.

❋ Mon-Wed 10-7, Thurs 10-8, Fri 10-7, Sat 9-7, Sun 12-6

unique
customised
clothing

The Lowry Outlet Mall

Manchester's only outlet mall, with 5 stores on two floors and up to 50% off shopping all year round. Discount retailers include famous names for clothing, as well as homeware and cosmetics companies.

To help recharge after shopping, the mall provides a 400-seat food court complete with cafés, food stalls and coffee bars. The mall also has a health and fitness centre and a seven-screen cinema. Various restaurants are open after hours, including Pond Quay (Chinese cuisine) and Lime (fresh, classic menu in an unpretentious setting).

i Salford Quays, Greater
Manchester M50 3AH
(0161) 848 1850
www.lowryoutletmall.com
Facilities: cafés, restaurants, disabled access, disabled parking, hearing impaired, visually impaired, licensed premises, internet access, passenger lift, toilets on premises, major credit cards accepted, parking on site.

* Shops: Mon-Wed and Fri 10-6, Thurs 10-8, Sat 10-7, Sun 11-5. The Centre: Mon-Fri 10am-1am, Sat 9am-1am, Sun 10am-11.30pm

Manchester Arndale

When it comes to city-centre shopping it is hard to beat Manchester Arndale, the largest of its kind in Britain. Recent redevelopment has provided an additional 300,000 square feet of retail space, along with a winter garden.

Inside you'll find a huge selection of shops and eateries, from leading high street names to dozens of smaller, stylish specialists – and all under one roof. Set in a purpose-built market hall, the brand new Manchester Arndale Market is one of the highlights of Manchester's retail havens – open seven days a week.

i Market Street,
Manchester M4 3AQ
T (0161) 833 9851
www.manchesterarndale.com
Facilities: cafés, restaurants, disabled access (Shopmobility offers free loan of wheelchairs and motorised chairs), information point, toilets on premises, passenger lifts, major credit cards taken, parking nearby.

* Mon-Sat 9-8, Sun 11-5

up to 50% off shopping all year round

Manchester Craft & Design Centre

Manchester Craft and Design Centre is a unique organisation comprising 16 retail/studio spaces, an excellent café and a rolling programme of exhibitions from leading national and international craftspeople.

Located in the central Northern Quarter, the Craft and Design Centre is at the hub of a growing innovative and artistic community. It is one of the few places in the UK open to the public where contemporary goods are both individually produced and sold on the premises.

Formerly the Smithfield Victorian fish market and crowned with a huge glass roof, the Centre now houses two floors of shops ranging from jewellery, ceramics and textiles to furniture and clothing design.

i 17 Oak Street, Northern Quarter, Manchester M4 5JD

T (0161) 832 4274
www.craftanddesign.com
Facilities: café-restaurant, disabled access, toilets on premises, information point, major credit cards taken, parking nearby.

❋ Mon-Sat 10-5.30

Selfridges

Selfridges is the definitive shopping destination in Manchester – world famous for its innovative window displays, and with a stylish mix of ingredients ranging from furniture and fashion to beauty and fine food.

The second of two Selfridges stores to appear in Manchester, this one is set across five spectacular floors on Exchange Square – each designed by an internationally renowned architect. A one-stop shop for exclusive brands and quality foods.

The other branch of Selfridges is located at the Trafford Centre (see below).

i 1 Exchange Square, Manchester M3 1BD

T 0870 837 7377
www.selfridges.com
Facilities: café, restaurant, disabled access, regular live entertainment, passenger lift, major credit cards accepted, parking nearby.

❋ Mon-Fri 10-8, Sat 9-8, Sun 11-5

the
definitive
shopping
destination

Trafford Centre

Situated just five miles outside Manchester city centre, visitors have the choice of 230 stores along three miles of granite and marble boulevards. As a whole, the Trafford Centre is the largest indoor shopping centre in Britain.

Stores range from all the favourite high street names to designer and high fashion outlets along Regent Crescent (including the first Selfridges to appear outside London).

The Trafford Centre's leisure and dining area – The Orient – hosts 36 restaurants and fast food eateries. The Centre is also home to the Odeon 20-screen cinema, one of the largest in the UK.

i Trafford Centre,
Manchester M17 8AA

T (0161) 749 1717
www.traffordcentre.co.uk
Facilities: cafés, restaurants, disabled access, hearing impaired, visually impaired, disabled parking, children's play area, parent and toddler spaces, passenger lift, toilets on premises, cycle storage available, free parking on site.

❋ Shops: Mon-Fri 10-10, Sat 10-8, Sun 12-6, Bank Holidays 10-8. Restaurants & entertainment: Mon-Thurs 10am-midnight, Fri-Sat 10am-3am, Sun 11am-midnight

Triangle

The Triangle Shopping Centre is situated opposite Selfridges, in Exchange Square – the new retail heart of Manchester. Fashion, food and drink, health and beauty, plus a good deal of exclusive brands – all these and more can be found at the Triangle Shopping Centre, open seven days a week.

Shops to be found inside the Centre include Green & Benz Contemporary Platinum, Karen Millen, Jigsaw, Vicki Martin, Zinc Bar & Grill, and Wrapit.

i Exchange Square,
Manchester, M4 3TR

T (0161) 834 8961
www.thetriangle.co.uk
Facilties: cafés, restaurants, disabled access, visually impaired, parent and toddler spaces, passenger lift, licensed premises, major credit cards accepted, toilets on premises, parking nearby.

❋ Mon-Wed 10-6, Thurs-Sat 10-7, Sun 11-5

✪ Speciality Markets

Manchester is home to a fascinating range of speciality and seasonal markets, with local retailers offering everything from handmade arts and crafts to jewellery and local farmers' produce. Whether it's the Fine Food Market on St Ann's Square, the German or Dutch markets (selling a wide range of beer, wine, food and crafts) or the Irish Festival Market... you're sure to find it all here in Manchester.

Christmas Markets

Held every year as a celebration of the festive season, the Christmas Markets incorporate a traditional German Market, a European Market, and an Arts and Crafts Market. St Ann's Square is transformed into a glittering winter wonderland with brightly lit traditional wooden chalets packed full of unusual Christmas gifts.

Meanwhile right in the heart of the city Albert Square is transformed into a bustling European marketplace with gifts galore. The stalls sell a variety of crafts and traditional Christmas gifts and decorations, such as handmade Christmas tree baubles and wooden toys. There are lots of treats to be enjoyed, including spicy pickles, hot chestnuts, delicious marzipan stollen and warming Gluhwein – sure to bring a rosy glow to your cheeks. You'll also find French cheeses and charcuterie, Dutch plants and bulbs, Christmas trees, Belgian chocolates, homemade chutney, pickles, aromatic oils, jewellery, decorative pottery and glassware. The Manchester Christmas Markets are rightly considered to be among the best in Europe.

- ℹ️ Albert Square, St Ann's Square and Exchange Street
- 🚊 Metrolink stations in St Peter's Square or Piccadilly Gardens
- ❄️ Mid-November to Christmas Mon-Sat 10-9, Sun 10-6

Dutch Market

Visitors to St Ann's Square in Manchester may be forgiven for thinking they are in Holland as they walk among flowers, windmills and clogs. Blue Delf pottery, white ceramics, around 20 different types of farmhouse-made cheeses and delicacies are all on sale. Try the deliciously named stroopwafels (a biscuit waffle with a caramel centre), poffertjes (pancakes made with shredded potatoes), karertkes (mini pancakes served with syrup, chocolate and/or liqueurs) or speculaas (Dutch biscuits with cinnamon).

Crafts from Holland include woksten (woodwork), hand-blown glass figurines and ornaments. The Dutch Market is also one of the UK's leading suppliers of fresh cut flowers, with trailing geranium, climbing jasmine and sweet williams offering inspiration to gardeners. For the more adventurous, calistemon (bottle brush), passion flower and japanese willow are also on sale. After a hard day's shopping, go Dutch and treat yourself to an imported beer in the square.

- ℹ️ St Ann's Square
- 🚊 Metrolink stations in St Peter's Square or Piccadilly Gardens
- ❄️ Opening dates and times to be confirmed

Farmers' Market

Because stallholders at the Farmers' Market are all farmers themselves, discerning customers are able to learn exactly how the food they are about to buy has been produced.

The market contains approximately 25 stalls bringing together farmers from across the North West. The produce available includes fresh vegetables such as carrots dug from the soil the night before, meats (ostrich, wild boar, pork, venison, lamb, beef, hams and sausages), turkey, chicken and fish (smoked salmon, trout and kippers). There are jams and honey, farm-baked cakes and pies, farmhouse chocolates, a vast range of cheeses, butter and dairy products, free range eggs, herbs and spices, marinated olives, sundried tomatoes, and fine English wines and liqueurs. There are also a number of hand-crafted consumables such as locally grown flowers and bedding plants.

- *i* Piccadilly Gardens, near the statue of Queen Victoria
- 🚋 Metrolink station in Piccadilly Gardens
- ✹ From 8.30am Fri-Sat on the second and fourth Saturday of each month

Fashion Market

If you are looking for individual pieces of clothing that combine elegance, high quality materials and workmanship – all at affordable prices – then pop along to the latest addition to Manchester's market scene. The Fashion Market is held every Saturday on Tib Street in the Northern Quarter. It is one of the first dedicated designer fashion markets in the North West.

The market aims to give budding designers a leg up the retail ladder, whilst giving the shopper the chance to buy original clothes, bags, purses, hats and jewellery. The emphasis is firmly on design and creativity, giving browsers the chance to buy one-off designs at reasonable prices, whilst supporting Manchester's fledgling talent. As a weekly fixture, the fashion market will complement the now well established flower market, which sells blooms and plants every Thursday, Friday and Saturday in the award-winning Piccadilly Gardens, from 10am until 6pm.

- *i* Tib Street, adjacent to Debenhams
- 🚋 Metrolink stop outside Debenhams department store on Market Street
- ✹ Saturday 10-5

marinated olives and sundried tomatoes

Retail Therapy

Fine Food Market

The introduction of the Manchester Fine Food Market in 2006 provides visitors with a place to buy a wide variety of locally produced fresh foods, including speciality meats, cheeses, breads, chutneys, pickles, black puddings, wild boar, ostrich, ice cream, bottled beers, sloe gin and smoked foods (fish, cheese, meats and poultry).

The overall aim of the market is to bring a variety of the best foods farmed and produced in the North West right into the city centre. Fancy lunch? Then pop down to the market and taste the food of your choice at the various market restaurants. The Port of Lancaster Smokehouse is a good example of the sort of traders that the market attracts.

Based near the River Lune in Lancaster, the smokehouse sources wild salmon and local game, poultry and meat for smoking on site.

- *i* St Ann's Square
- 🚍 Metrolink stations in St Peter's Square or Piccadilly Gardens
- 🌟 Opening dates and times to be confirmed; usually open in October

Food & Drink Market

The excellent Food & Drink Market returns each year to complement the autumnal Food & Drink Festival – a banquet of gourmet activities, including food and wine tastings, celebrity chef demonstrations, charity cook-offs, and of course the wonderful Food & Drink Market itself. The market offers up the finest food and drink wares from local areas as well as elsewhere in Britain, allowing the city-centre shopper to experience the best there is in regional produce.

The market often includes a restaurant stall offering an à la carte selection of delectables for both lunch and dinner. With top chefs providing the cuisine, this really is one not to miss.

Meanwhile, the festival lays on a belly-full of events to keep the mouth watering throughout the season. Make sure you stop by the International Food Pavilion, where the city's best restaurants serve a hot, quick and fast take on their usual style of cuisine.

- 🌟 Every autumn, opening dates and times to be confirmed
- *i* St Ann's Square
- 🚍 Metrolink stations in St Peter's Square or Piccadilly Gardens

locally produced fresh food

German Market

Each year, the German Market and Beer Garden returns to fill up Albert Square with regional delights such as schnitzel, sauerkraut and malt beer, all served in traditional wooden chalets. A host of traders arrive in Manchester from Germany and set up stall in front of the Victorian splendour of Manchester Town Hall – all of them hoping to tempt passers-by with food and drink that is unavailable elsewhere in the city.

A trip to the German market would not be complete without a Bratwurst – either spiced, cheesy or traditional. You can also expect a huge 'swinggrill' serving a range of juicy sausages and steaks. For many, the highlight is the Bavarian beer house, which sells a selection of fine brewed beers.

Alternatively, stop by the pancake house (turning out traditional German pancakes), the coffee shop, the bakery, the wine house, or the craft traders who sell the likes of cuckoo clocks, glassware and jewellery.

i   Albert Square, in front of Manchester Town Hall

🚃   Metrolink station in St Peter's Square

❋   Opening dates and times to be confirmed

Irish Festival Market

The Irish Festival Market is held each year in celebration of St Patrick's Day. Retailers offer a huge variety of goods and wares direct from Ireland, including arts and crafts, gifts and traditional food, such as the best in Irish cheeses. The Irish Market is itself part of the much larger Irish Festival – a celebration of all things Irish, which brings together performers, workshops, and ceilidhs from across Britain.

First launched in 1996, the festival has gone on to become one of the biggest Irish festivals in Europe. Levenshulme village – home to the biggest Irish community outside London – turns green when it stages its annual 'Irish Fleadh', featuring dozens of events and hundreds of performers, most free of charge.

Other highlights include the Irish Festival Parade, which begins at the Irish World Heritage Centre and winds its way towards the centre of Manchester.

i   Outside the Town Hall on Albert Square

🚃   Metrolink station in St Peter's Square

❋   Opening dates and times to be confirmed

a celebration of all things Irish

Manchester's Quarters

Northern Quarter

Home to creative agencies, art galleries, fashion designers, independent boutiques, and quirky bars and restaurants, the Northern Quarter is Manchester's funky, alternative district.

Sited between Piccadilly and Ancoats, the Northern Quarter retains a unique character and charm – one set to continue through its ongoing development and regeneration.

Whist retaining its bohemian character, the Northern Quarter is nevertheless growing in popularity and becoming the new vibrant area to live-work-play among many age groups. In recent years, the quarter has become a contemporary and inspirational extension to the core of city-centre Manchester.

Browse vintage boutiques, cool record shops and contemporary art galleries selling amazing one-off pieces. Or disappear into the maze-like bazaar of shops at Afflecks Palace, its outer walls splashed with Mancunian references. Inside, you'll find four floors packed with independent retail stores selling everything from kitsch to cool, vintage to chic. Be sure to stop for a cup of tea on the top floor and enjoy the view over Manchester's city centre.

This is undoubtedly Manchester's most creative quarter, so keep your ear to the ground and you might catch wind of an extraordinary one-off event, or the next up-and-coming artist exhibiting at one of the many independent galleries.

However you spend your time in the Northern Quarter be sure to round off your day at one of the many quirky and interesting bars and restaurants.

★ Highlights
Afflecks Palace
Fashion Market
Craft & Design Centre

from kitsch to cool

The Gay Village

Manchester's gay district is no more than one square mile in size, but its importance and impact as a spiritual home for European 'queer' culture is enormous.

It is the home of Canal Street, Manto, Queer as Folk, and Manchester Pride, and has grown since the late 1980s to become one of the most ebullient and exciting inner-city areas in the UK.

Situated along the Bridgewater Canal, between Princess Street and Aytoun Street, the Gay Village is home to a collection of classy glass-fronted bars and stylish restaurants. Its community vibe is also enhanced by a series of gay-friendly businesses, ranging from doctors to hairdressers. Meanwhile, contained within the neighbourhood's old warehouses and buildings are some of the most sought-after luxury apartments in Manchester.

The centre of it all is Canal Street, which comes to life after dark thanks to a diverse range of bars, cafés and clubs. There's probably nowhere else quite like it in Europe.

The Village as a whole comes into its own during August, when Manchester Pride brings a carnival atmosphere to the streets. Manchester Pride is an annual celebration of gay culture, attracting a quarter of a million visitors to the city for ten days of celebrations, music, performance and sport.

★ Highlights
Canal Street
Out in the Past Heritage Trail
Taurus Bar & Restaurant

Pride brings a carnival atmosphere

Chinatown

Manchester's Chinese community is vital to the social fabric of the modern city. Indeed, Manchester's Chinatown is often acknowledged as one of the largest and most vibrant Chinatowns outside China itself.

The magnificent Imperial Chinese Arch, which greets you as you enter Chinatown, is the neighbourhood's primary landmark and the only one of its kind to be found in Europe. For a temporary escape from the city, visitors can explore the two pavilions beside the arch, set amongst ornamental gardens.

Pass through the archway into Chinatown, and you're soon bombarded with the smells of dumplings, teas and spices as you walk past an array of bakeries, restaurants and herbalists.

As well as gift shops, food shops, clothing stores and markets, Chinatown is packed full of restaurants serving a seemingly limitless choice of Asian cuisines – thanks largely to the neighbourhood's diverse ethnic mix. While the predominant cuisines on offer are Cantonese and Pekingese, you will also stumble across restaurants serving Malaysian, Thai, Singaporean, Japanese and Nepalese food.

Be sure to visit one of the many supermarkets and bakeries nestling between the throng of restaurants; the honey buns at Ho's Bakery are simply to die for. The best time to visit Chinatown is of course during the Chinese New Year festivities, when thousands of spectators gather to watch the biggest dancing dragon in Europe.

★ Highlights
Imperial Chinese Arch
Manchester Art Gallery
Wide choice of Asian cuisine

Castlefield

With its series of interlocking canals, Castlefield is a picturesque corner of the city, buzzing with bars, canal barges and eateries – especially during August when the free music festival D:Percussion is held.

Castlefield goes back a long way. When the Romans took control of the North of England during the AD 70s, they built a series of forts, including one in Castlefield. The fort was abandoned when the Romans withdrew from Britain around AD 410, and the surrounding area returned to the wilds. By the Middle Ages, the area was known locally as the 'Castle-in-the-Field' – later condensed to 'Castlefield'.

It is not only Roman heritage that draws visitors to Castlefield. The neighbourhood also contains a wealth of industrial heritage, from historic railway viaducts and canal systems to fascinating museums. As such, the Castlefield area has been designated Britain's first Urban Heritage Park.

Most of the once-derelict industrial buildings in Castlefield have now been renovated or restored to their former glory, and numerous archaeological digs have revealed the early history of the city.

For many visitors the primary attractions are the boat trips along the canals, the waterside pubs, the pleasant walks and the excellent range of restaurants.

Visit the Castlefield Visitors' Centre on Liverpool Road for more information about what the neighbourhood has to offer.

★ Highlights
Open Air Arena
Castlefield Carnival
Canal barge trips

Britain's first Urban Heritage Park

Manchester's Quarters

Millennium Quarter

The area around Manchester Cathedral in the city centre has been resurrected as the Millennium Quarter, a careful blend of historic buildings and striking modern architecture.

The skyline in the new Millennium Quarter has been transformed by the 21st-century steel and glass structures of Exchange Square, housing top-class restaurants, bars, cafés and nightclubs.

Among the new buildings stands Urbis, a spectacular mirrored-glass building that throws light onto the surrounding streets. The building houses a unique museum: on passing through the entrance, visitors are whisked to the fourth floor in a funicular-like elevator where the experiences of entering a city for the first time are recreated. As a whole, the museum explores a spectrum of world cities (including Manchester) and the people who live in them. See p.34 for more on Urbis.

The lush green beauty of the new Cathedral Gardens adds a softer, more genteel, face to this ultra-modern quarter. A stroll across the street from here brings you to the magnificent Printworks, a state-of-the-art entertainment complex housed in what was formerly the largest printing facility in Europe. Today, the Printworks is a Gotham City-type structure with an indoor street and a range of bars, restaurants, clubs and cinema screens.

The Millennium Quarter is also home to the MEN Arena – the largest indoor arena in Europe – and the Triangle shopping centre, a wonderful reinvention of the old Corn Exchange.

★ Highlights

Urbis

Printworks

MEN Arena

Gotham City-type structure

Piccadilly

The square at Piccadilly Gardens is currently the transport hub of Manchester, though the quarter is dominated by the gardens themselves, which represent the largest green space within the bounds of the city centre.

Built on the site of the old Manchester Royal Infirmary, the gardens lie to the south of the Northern Quarter and east of Market Street.

The whole area has been reinvented as a contemporary urban space, with open lawns, fountains and pavilion buildings – perfect for a short break. Piccadilly is also home to the Piccadilly Railway Station, which originally dates back to 1842 and retains a few of the original iron sheds with their decorative cast iron columns.

Eminent Japanese architect Tadao Ando revamped the main square in 2001 and 2002 to include more green space.

The square is surrounded by buildings that span the ages of modern Manchester – from old Victorian warehouses and shops dating from the Industrial Revolution (when Manchester served as the cotton capital of Britain) to the new office block developments that are part of Piccadilly Garden's regeneration. Dominating them all is the huge complex of Piccadilly Plaza. The original building, which frequently invoked mixed reactions in locals, was remodelled by Leslie Jones Architects in 2001 and 2002.

★ Highlights
Piccadilly Gardens
New bars and restaurants
Queen Victoria statue

reinvented as a contemporary urban space

Manchester's Quarters

Deansgate and Market Street

Deansgate is one of Manchester's most prominent addresses – home to Britain's oldest department store, Kendals (now House of Fraser).

Upmarket bars, restaurants and boutiques have sprung up in the vicinity, while the beautifully sculpted green space of Parsonage Gardens is a haven from the bustle of the city.

To the east of Deansgate, the shopper's paradise truly begins, with Market Street and Manchester Arndale – the largest retail centre of its kind in Britain, complete with a market hall and the new Winter Gardens. Just south of here, the area around King Street and St Ann's Square plays host to a string of designer boutiques.

One of the cultural highlights of this quarter is the Royal Exchange Theatre, which is recognised as a major focal point of contemporary craftwork in the North West. The theatre itself hosts a varied programme of plays and other special events, and the building also houses a bookshop, brasserie and foyer gallery.

The quarter's other major focal point is St Ann's Square and the markets it plays host to throughout the year. This is the place to come for the finest local and regional produce – sold at the stalls of the Fine Foods Market and the Food & Drink Market. The square also hosts the seasonal Dutch Market and the festive Christmas Markets, which transform much of the city centre each year.

★ Highlights
Manchester Arndale
Royal Exchange Theatre
Markets on St Ann's Square

shopper's
paradise
truly
begins

82

Manchester's Quarters

Petersfield

Also known as the 'Conference Quarter', Petersfield is the newly developed area surrounding the Manchester International Convention Centre (MICC), the magnificent G-Mex Centre (formerly Central Station) and Bridgewater Hall.

The area is also packed with bars and pubs, and has developed into one of Manchester's favourite night spots.

Music lovers will be drawn to the famed Hallé Symphony Orchestra, who are in residence at the stunning Bridgewater Hall – a state-of-the-art 2,400 seat auditorium with a magnificent Marcussen pipe organ. Concerts here range from classical and jazz through to world and popular music.

For a night out on the town, Deansgate Locks is the place to be, with the railway arches behind the G-Mex providing a fantastic collection of canal-side bars. This is where the city's in-crowd like to hang out.

The area around Peter Street is also home to stylish bars and clubs, though with more of a mainstream bent.

On the northern edge of this quarter, on St Peter's Square, you'll find the Library Theatre Company, an intimate 312-seat basement space with an enviable reputation for its challenging productions of the work of American playwrights.

To the south, just across the canal, is Cornerhouse, one of the UK's leading centres for film and visual arts. Inside you'll find contemporary art galleries and three cinema screens ranged over three floors, along with a bar, café and bookshop.

Peel off south onto Oxford Road, and you enter an area often described as the 'Southern Quarter' – the stomping ground of Manchester's large student population.

★ Highlights
Bridgewater Hall
Deansgate Locks
Cornerhouse

fantastic collection of canal-side bars

84
Gay Manchester

Embracing all lesbian, gay, bisexual and transgender life, Manchester is one of the world's most gay-friendly cities. A vibrant and dynamic metropolis, Manchester has long been a pioneer of the free and open expression of sexuality. With the very best in culture, nightlife, food and drink, entertainment and shopping – Manchester awaits newcomers with open arms.

Manchester's industrial legacy is stitched into the fabric of the city, but if the word 'industrial' brings the bleak and grey to mind, think again. Manchester combines the old and new with flair and imagination. New iconic buildings sit alongside Victorian grandeur housing everything from stylish hotels and apartments to bars, clubs and restaurants.

In Manchester's museums and galleries, you can discover the art and culture not only of the local area, but also of Britain in general. In fact, Manchester is a major international centre for the arts. Theatres and venues large and small offer the best in drama, music, performance and film. Look out for cultural festivals, too, which celebrate food and drink, literature, comedy, cinema and more.

As this is the fashion capital of the North of England, you'll want to put some time aside for browsing the shops and boutiques. Flagship stores, exclusive labels, independent designers and all your favourite high street chains are all open late, every day of the year. What's more, the compact dimensions of the city mean that negotiating the different shopping quarters is a breeze.

Manchester also hosts free art, drama, live music, parades and street performances in the public squares and spaces. Don't miss Manchester Pride in August each year for a celebration of all things lesbian, gay, bisexual and transgender.

With so much to keep you busy, you'll need to refuel at regular intervals. And Manchester packs some punch when it comes to food and drink. There are more than 30 different kinds of cuisine on offer across the city, along with a community of world-class chefs. For quality local produce and continental goods from across Europe, visit Manchester's many speciality markets. If you're saving the pennies, don't miss the unique atmosphere of Chinatown and the Curry Mile.

one of the world's most gay-friendly cities

The less you spend on eating out, the more you have for Manchester's fantastic nightlife. Pubs and clubs are scattered right across the city – try Deansgate Locks or the Northern Quarter – but the main focus has to be the Gay Village. Canal Street is the heart of it all, a 400-metre stretch of bars, pubs, clubs, cafés and restaurants. Amongst the Rainbow Flag pavement mosaics, people from across the spectrum of lesbian, gay, bisexual and transgender life party long into the night, seven days a week.

Manchester's Gay Village is a home from home, wherever you're from. Old school gay pubs such as The Rembrandt and Churchills nestle alongside trendy bars such as Spirit and Queer. Indulge yourself with a delicious cocktail in the sophisticated setting of Taurus or meander through the gothic labyrinth of Via Fossa. The award-winning club Vanilla offers something for the ladies, whilst Company bar attracts grizzly bears and leather chaps. Don't miss Poptastic every Tuesday and Saturday at Mutz Nutz – this popular club has two rooms, so you can choose

between cheesy pop and indie tunes. Dance your socks off at Cruz 101, or for serious clubbers, catch the after-hours party at Essential.

And remember, gay-friendly bars and clubs are not confined only to the Gay Village. Enjoy a glass of wine in the laid-back bar at the Malmaison, or take the express lift to the stylish Cloud 23 bar at the Hilton Manchester Deansgate: the views across the city are spectacular. Make sure you discover the creative and funky Northern Quarter, too. Here you will find independent bars and clubs such as Socio Rehab and Mint Lounge, the latter offering some of the best intimate live gigs from home-grown talent and international artists.

Feel welcome, be proud and have a great time: you're in Manchester.

creative
and funky
Northern
Quarter

Gay Manchester

⚜ Key Events

Manchester Pride

The only place to be during the last few weeks of August is celebrating at Manchester Pride – the city's annual lesbian, gay, bisexual and transgender (LGBT) festival. Held over ten days, Manchester Pride has become much more than just a party. It promises something for everyone with a host of activities including a film festival, sports events, arts and entertainment, and lots of partying. So, whether your idea of a good time is to find out about gay heritage, or to dance your rocks off until the sun comes up – you're sure to find lots to do.

- ⚜ August (exact dates to be confirmed; check website)
- 🚍 Metrolink Station in Piccadilly Gardens
  www.manchesterpride.com

Pride Games

Part of the ten-day celebration of Manchester Pride, the Games aim to create, encourage and support opportunities for LGBT people to enjoy and participate in leisure activities. The broad programme of events includes athletics, a sailing regatta, a big ballroom event at a prestigious location, and a dazzling 'Sport For All' line-up.

- ⚜ August (exact dates to be confirmed; check website)
- 𝒊 City centre
- 🚍 Metrolink Station in Piccadilly Gardens
  www.pridegames.org

Queerupnorth Festival

The UK's original gay arts festival is Europe's biggest celebration of everything queer and features outstanding theatre, inspired performance and the biggest international collection of gay cinema ever to hit Manchester. The festival celebrates the very best in arts and artists who explore LGBT issues in their work.

- ⚜ May (exact dates to be confirmed; check website)
- 𝒊 citywide
  www.queerupnorth.com

Great British Bear Bash

This world famous Bear get-together is held over the first weekend of May every year and offers an attitude-free event. The event attracts people from all over the world and grows in popularity with every year.

- ⚜ May (exact dates to be confirmed; check website)
- 𝒊 The Gay Village, city centre
  www.manbears.co.uk

⚜ Choice Bar-Restaurants

Eden (££)

Eden is a contemporary restaurant and bar situated in the heart of Manchester's Gay Village. Since opening its doors in 2002, Eden has earned a reputation for combining quality food, exceptional service and a fantastic atmosphere to create an unforgettable night out.

ℹ 3 Brazil Street,
  Manchester M1 3PJ
T (0161) 237 9852
  www.edenbar.co.uk

Gaia (££)

See p.63, under 'Bars'.

ℹ 46 Sackville Street,
  Manchester M1 3WF
T (0161) 228 1002

Malmaison Brasserie (££)

Malmaison is an award-winning hotel with an Art Nouveau interior and a new-look brasserie and bar. Located in a former textile warehouse from 1904-6, the food is mouthwateringly tasty and wholesome, with 'prix fixe' menus that change daily.

ℹ Piccadilly,
  Manchester M1 3AQ
T (0161) 278 1000
  www.malmaison.com

Manto Bar (££)

A big glass-fronted bar and diner that revolutionised gay Manchester and more or less brought the Village out of the closet when it opened in the early 1990s.

ℹ 46 Canal Street,
  Manchester M1 3WD
T (0161) 236 2667
  www.mantobar.com

Obsidian Bar & Restaurant (£££)

See p.29, under 'Restaurants'.

ℹ Arora International Hotel,
  18-24 Princess Street,
  Manchester M1 4LY
T (0161) 236 4348
  www.obsidianmanchester.co.uk

Queer (£)

Queer is an exclusive gay lifestyle café-bar on Canal Street offering a modern, contemporary space at the heart of Manchester's Gay Village. Chilled music is played during the daytime, and this transmutes to a full on club in the evenings.

ℹ 4 Canal Street,
  Manchester M1 3HE
T (0161) 228 1360
  www.queer-manchester.com

Taurus

See p.62, under 'Restaurants'.

ℹ 1 Canal Street,
  Manchester M1 3HE
T (0161) 236 4593
  www.taurus-bar.co.uk

Art
Nouveau
interior

Tribeca (££)

A chic and vibrant city-centre bar with a distinct and sophisticated New York air. The bar offers a relaxed atmosphere by day, and a buzzy, vibrant scene by night. The attached B.E.D. Bar is an underground ultra lounge and restaurant where you can dine and recline on full-sized beds.

i 50 Sackville Street,
   Manchester M1 3WF

T (0161) 236 8300
   www.tribeca-bar.co.uk

Vanilla (£)

A famous lesbian bar and club, open until 2am all week. Serves food and has regular themed nights. Since opening in 1998, Vanilla has won many awards for its total dedication and commitment to the lesbian scene, not only in Manchester but throughout Britain.

i 39-41 Richmond Street,
   Manchester M1 3WB

T (0161) 228 2727
   www.vanillagirls.co.uk

Velvet (££)

This award-winning café-bar pioneered the 'New York Loft' ambience in Manchester. Known for its excellent food, eclectic music style and Sunday Jazz, Velvet has quickly earned a reputation as one of the places to drink, eat and be seen in Manchester.

i 2 Canal Street,
   Manchester M1 3HE

T (0161) 236 9003

'New York loft' ambience

Admission prices for the following parks and gardens are graded according to the price of a single adult admission:
£ = under £5; ££ = £5-£10; £££ = over £10

Bramall Hall Park (£)

Set in beautiful parkland, Bramall Hall is a superb example of a Cheshire black and white timber-framed manor house, dating from the 14th century. Together, the house and grounds are a marvellous historic record spanning six centuries (the original manor house even features in the Domesday Book).

Today, the Victorian kitchen, boudoir and servants' quarters give a unique insight into the lives of the families and servants who have resided at Bramall Hall over the centuries. Look out for the spectacular plaster ceilings, the wall paintings and the array of furniture and artwork from different periods of history.

The house is set within 70 acres of tranquil parkland, all of which has been landscaped in the style of Capability Brown. The park features two lakes, a series of woodland walks, gardens and a toddlers' play area.

- *i* Bramall, Stockport SK7 3NX
- **T** (0161) 485 3708
  www.bramallhall.org.uk
- + *Family friendly, guide dogs welcome, parking on site, toilets on site, open all year*

Chorlton Water Park (free)

Chorlton Water Park is a local nature reserve surrounded by woodland, with plenty of footpaths, picnic tables and play areas for children.

Set on the site of the old Barlow Hall Farm, the lake is well stocked with coarse fish and has 80 fixed fishing platforms, with those on the south side of the lake accessible for wheelchair users. During the winter months, the lake becomes an important refuge for wildlife – notably as an over-wintering site for migrating wildfowl. At other times of year, the lake accommodates a variety of water based activities including dinghy sailing, canoeing, windsurfing and model boating.

The paths around the lake are suitable for pram-pushers, wheelchair users, cyclists and horse riders. From a peaceful stroll to a strenuous run around the orienteering course, the park has something for everyone.

- *i* Maitland Avenue, Manchester M21 7WH
- **T** (0161) 881 5639
- + *Disabled access, family friendly, toilets on site, free car park, open all year*

historic
record
spanning
six
centuries

Dunham Massey House & Gardens (££)

Surrounding the magnificent 18th-century house, the garden at Dunham Massey is a great plantsman's garden with interesting historic features such as an orangery, pump house, Victorian bank house and the remains of an Elizabethan Mount. The 250 acres of parkland are also home to an ancient herd of fallow deer.

Undoubtedly one of the North West's great gardens, Dunham Massey is a place to return to through the year – stunning in any season. Meanwhile, the house itself is home to the finest collection of Huguenot silver in the country.

The varied site and acid soil hosts a wide range of unusual shade and moisture-loving plants including giant Chinese lilies, Himalayan blue poppies and rare late-flowering azaleas – all set amongst manicured lawns, mixed borders and cool woodland.

i Altrincham, Cheshire WA14 4SJ
(0161) 941 1025
www.nationaltrust.org.uk
Disabled access & parking, baby changing facilities, toilets on site, park open all year

Fletcher Moss Botanical Gardens (free)

This 21-acre park was acquired as a gift from Alderman Fletcher Moss in 1914. Renowned for their botanical beauty, the gardens contain many antiquated and unusual plants and flowers.

The park has retained many of its original features, such as the rock and heather gardens, and the orchid houses situated in the Parsonage Gardens. The latter comprise a high walled garden of rare trees, roses, shrubs, plants and herbaceous borders. Look out for the old yew tree, which is the site of Fletcher Moss's pet cemetery.

The main feature of the adjacent Botanical Gardens is the lovely rock garden with its rare plants, pools and waterfalls set on a south-facing slope. Together, the Botanical Gardens and Parsonage Gardens form a picturesque, tranquil haven for visitors, complete with a café serving home-made cakes. The park also provides an excellent setting for the annual summer Park Play Performance.

i Millgate Lane Didsbury, Manchester M20 2RZ
T (0161) 434 1877
+ *Café-restaurant, family friendly, parking nearby, open all year*

one of the North West's great gardens

Haigh Hall & Country Park (free)

Once the home of Earls and Lords, Haigh Hall is surrounded by 250 acres of park and woodland, with magnificent views across the Douglas Valley.

Built between 1827 and 1840, Haigh Hall was for many years the ancestral home of the Lindsay family – the Earls of Crawford and Balcarres. The hall and its grounds were bought by Wigan Corporation in 1947 and now make up one of the region's most beautiful country parks.

The adjoining country park is an enjoyable day out for all the family. Facilities include a model village, play area, miniature railway, 'ladybird' ride, mini-golf, craft gallery, information centre, gift shop and café.

The adjoining 18-hole golf course is probably one of the most scenic and challenging courses in the area. Best of all, enjoy the tranquility of the stunning parkland, woodland and plantations. Haigh Hall is also a venue for conferences, meetings, dinners, wedding receptions and craft fairs.

ℹ Copperas Lane, Haigh, Wigan WN2 1PE

T (01942) 832 895
www.haighhall.net

+ *Café-restaurant, family friendly, disabled parking and access, guide dogs welcome, visually impaired, toilets on site, open all year*

Heaton Park (free)

Heaton Park is one of the largest municipal parks in Europe and was part of the estate of the Earls of Wilton. At 640 acres, the park forms 25% of the green space in Manchester.

Set on the city outskirts, the park nestles in the foothills of the Pennines, ringed by the former mill towns of Oldham, Rochdale and Bury. Its rolling scenery provides an attractive setting for a wide range of leisure activities. It is also a memorable backdrop for outdoor events, family fun days, workshops, bonfire and firework displays, theatrical productions and concerts.

Listed Grade II on English Heritage's register of historic parks and gardens, the park contains eight protected structures including the Grade I listed Heaton Hall, a James Wyatt house which was described by Pevsner as one of the finest houses of its period in the country. The park and hall retain many of their original features.

ℹ Middleton Road, Higher Blackley, Manchester M25 2SW

T (0161) 773 1085

+ *Disabled access, family friendly, toilets on site, free car park, open all year*

25% of the green space in Manchester

Hollingworth Lake Country Park (free)

Hollingworth Lake Country Park provides the perfect gateway to the beautiful open moorlands of the South Pennines. Lying at the foot of Blackstone Edge, there are a wide variety of footpaths and trails leading off into the surrounding countryside. A regular programme of guided walks, cycle trips and outdoor activities are organised by Rochdale's Countryside Service, with something for all abilities.

A focal point for visitors is Hollingworth Lake itself, built in 1801 to supply water to the Rochdale Canal. The lake was used by Captain Webb as a training ground for the first Cross Channel swim and it remains a thriving centre for watersports, including sailing, canoeing and trips on the 47-seater pleasure launch 'Lady Alice'.

Alternatively, call in at the hide to view the wide variety of birdlife in the nature reserve, or settle down at one of the picnic and play areas along the route.

i Rakewood Road, Littleborough, Rochdale OL15 0AQ

☎ (01706) 373 421

www.rochdale.gov.uk

+ *Café-restaurant, accessible with assistance, guide dogs welcome, baby changing facilities, toilets on site, parking on site*

Moses Gate Country Park (free)

Also known as Crompton Lodges, this 750-acre park is situated in the Croal Irwell Valley, three miles from Bolton town centre. The country park offers a diversity of habitats, supporting many different forms of wildlife. The 'Kingfisher' way-marked trail passes through the park on its journey down the Croal Irwell Valley. (The whole trail is 11 miles in length.)

The Moses Gate Country Park also offers a wide range of facilities and activities for visitors including walking trails, picnic areas, a bird hide, an orienteering trail and a bridleway for horse riding. Permits are available for fishing, canoeing, boating, and the use of model aircraft and model boats. Countryside rangers are available to work with groups and schools (booking required).

i Rock Hall Visitor Centre, Farnworth, Bolton BL4 7QN

☎ (01204) 334 343

+ *Disabled access, guide dogs welcome, disabled parking, family friendly, toilets on site, free car parking, open all year*

training ground for the first Cross Channel swim

Moss Bank Park (free)

Moss Bank Park combines a recreation park with a series of gardens and a zoo. The highlight is Animal World, which provides a free-living environment for everything from farm animals and chipmunks to wildfowl and tropical birds. The Butterfly House, meanwhile, features free-flying butterflies and moths in a tropical environment, as well as insects, spiders, reptiles and tropical plants. Admission to both the park and Animal World is free.

Moss Bank Park was originally used for the Ainsworth family's bleaching business and family residence. Other attractions within the Park include a miniature railway (which runs on summer weekends), a children's play area, a rock garden, an old English garden, tennis courts, pitches for football and cricket, a pitch-and-putt course, a bowling green and a café (open on summer weekends only).

- *i* Moss Bank Way,
  Bolton BL1 6NQ
- **T** (01204) 334 050
- **+** *Disabled access, family friendly, free parking, open all year*

Platt Fields Park (free)

Ideally situated in central Manchester, Platt Fields Park is set in 170 acres of grounds and is one of Manchester's major outdoor sites. The park was formally opened in May 1910 and was landscaped with the help of local people during a period of high unemployment. They inverted the Gore Brook and planted the banks with trees and shrubs.

The main feature of the park was the construction of a lake and island that covers a little over six acres. Other work included levelling the park and playing fields, formation of the bowling greens, tennis courts and bathing pool.

The park has three dedicated show fields that have a supported infrastructure for large-scale national and small-scale local events. Other facilities include two playgrounds, a series of gardens, a boating lake, a basketball court, a five-a-side pitch, a skatepark and a labyrinth.

- *i* Wilmslow Road, Rusholme,
  Manchester M14 6LA
- **T** (0161) 224 2902
- **+** *Café-restaurant, disabled access, parking on site, open all year*

a free-living
environment

Parks and Gardens

Smithills Country Park (free)

Set in 2,000 acres of woodland, farmland and moorland on the edge of the West Pennine Moors, Smithills Country Park offers superb views over Bolton and the surrounding area. It serves as an excellent destination for walkers, cyclists and horse riders, with guided trails, picnic areas and a small visitor centre. A series of excellent off-road bridleways provide a network of routes for mountain bikers and horse riders.

There are four self-guided tours around the park with leaflets available on each. Countryside Rangers are available to work with schools and groups (booking required). The park also includes Smithills Coaching House Restaurant, Smithills Hall and Smithills Open Farm. Smithills Hall is a beautiful 15th-century manor house set in formal grounds, while the farm gives children the chance to feed lambs, stroke rabbits and ride donkeys.

i Smithills Dean Road,
Bolton BL4 7NP

T (01204) 334 010

+ *Disabled parking, guide dogs welcome, free parking on site, open all year dawn till dusk*

Tatton Park (££)

Tatton Park constitutes England's most complete historic estate, with a mansion, 50-acre garden, traditional working farm, medieval Old Hall, and 1,000 acres of parkland including two lakes.

Tatton's open park offers trails, horse riding, fishing, an adventure playground, and the opportunity to spot abundant wildlife. Rare bird sightings are noted by the park rangers on the wildlife notice board. Herds of fallow deer wander freely across the park, while in summer sheep graze on the grasslands. It is a beautiful place with grand vistas, changing moods throughout the year and enough space to escape from today's hectic lifestyle.

The parkland hosts a number of Tatton's events including the award-winning Halle Fireworks and Light Spectacular concert by the side of Tatton Mere, and the RHS Flower Show at Tatton Park, which has already gained a national reputation.

i Knutsford,
Cheshire WA16 6QN

T (01625) 534 400
www.tattonpark.org.uk

+ *Café-restaurant, disabled parking and access, family friendly, parking on site, open all year*

Walkden Gardens (free)

Known locally as the 'Maze', due to the ingenious layout of the beech hedges, Walkden Gardens were inspired by the famous gardens of Hidcote Manor on the Gloucestershire-Warwickshire border.

Children delight in playing hide-and-seek among the hedges, which form a splendid backcloth to the numerous flower beds and shrubberies that have developed over the years. All of the paths that snake through the maze lead to interesting features, including a 25-metre-long laburnum arch, a fuchsia garden, a theatre lawn, a cherry walk and more.

Once known as the Moorside Nurseries, the original gardens were donated to Sale Borough Council by Harry Walkden for the purpose of developing them into an amusement park or botanical gardens. Recent restoration work has seen the gardens restored to their former glory, with plans afoot to host concerts, family fun days, nature walks and other activities.

i Derbyshire Road, Sale, Cheshire
www.salecommunityweb.co.uk/walkden.htm

+ *Free car parking*

Worthington Lakes Country Park (free)

The Worthington Lakes Country Park is an attractive area of woodland surrounding three reservoirs, with access to the Red Rock Cycle and Bridleway.

The lakes lie within the Douglas Valley, and are fed by the River Douglas which originates on the moors above Rivington. Their history spans back to the mid-1800s, when the river was diverted to create the reservoirs.

Today Worthington Lakes are part of a 50-acre country park, with a nature reserve, an Environmental Education Centre and fishing sites. A network of footpaths and picnic sites leading off from the lakes offer a variety of scenic views, while a trail designed for the visually impaired follows a mature tree-lined walkway. Fishing is allowed from mid-June through to mid-March and tickets are available from the visitor centre.

i Worthington, Standish, Wigan
T (01257) 425 550

+ *Accessible with assistance, no dogs allowed, open all year*

Alkrington Woods

Once part of the Alkrington Hall Estate, near Middleton in Greater Manchester, this area of mature woodland provides an ideal habitat for a wide range of flora and fauna.

Informal paths take the visitor through woodland along the banks of the River Irk and around the ponds and fishing lodges at Rhodes. Habitats include woodland, grassland, marsh, standing water and separate amenity areas.

The woodland here is easily accessible, with self-guided trails and full disabled access. Special events are sometimes hosted in and around the woods (check with the Rochdale Tourist Information Centre for more details, or visit www.rochdale.gov.uk). The 'Friends of Alkrington Woods' also run occasional conservation-based activities which help to sustain the woodland in its natural state – phone (01706) 350 459 for further details.

Dovestones Reservoir

Dovestones Reservoir occupies a stunning setting above the village of Greenfield in Greater Manchester. The reservoir was created as a water catchment for the surrounding area, but has since developed into a major tourist attraction, offering a number of picturesque walks among the surrounding landscapes.

High above the Dovestones Reservoir stand the Wimberry Rocks, popular with climbers and thought by some to be the most dramatic grit crag in the Peak District National Park. On another side of the reservoir is a group of small crags known locally as 'Indian's Head' (look for an upturned face).

The reservoir itself is said to have been named after a separate collection of stones on the skyline that resemble a dove. It is an easy walk to the reservoir from the village of Greenfield. Rolling moors, peat bogs and dry stone walls characterise the surrounding scenery.

★ Highlights
Fishing ponds
Mature woodland
Special events

★ Highlights
Wimberry Rocks
Stone formations
Circular walk

dramatic
grit crag

Out into the Countryside

Healey Dell

Situated two miles outside Rochdale town centre, on the way to Whitworth and Bacup, Healey Dell is a beauty spot and wildlife sanctuary rich in industrial archaeology.

Over the course of thousands of years, the River Spodden has carved its way through the surrounding woodlands, creating delightful scenery and spectacular waterfalls which once powered ancient corn, wool and cotton mills. A disused 19th-century railway line now serves as a nature trail, providing magnificent views from the top of a hundred-foot-high viaduct.

As a designated nature reserve, Healey Dell is a great place for spotting wildlife indigenous to England. Healey Dell also has a visitor centre where you'll find a permanent exhibition on the industrial heritage of the site. Guided walks are also available.

Huddersfield Narrow Canal

The Huddersfield Narrow Canal is famous for Standedge Tunnel, the longest, deepest and highest canal tunnel in the country, burrowing 645 feet beneath the Pennines for nearly three and a half miles.

In 2001 the tunnel was officially reopened by HRH The Prince of Wales after 50 years of neglect – an incredible feat of restoration set in motion by the Huddersfield Canal Society. The tunnel originally took 16 years to build at considerable cost of life and with the final section being overseen by renowned engineer Thomas Telford in 1811.

A journey along the 20-mile canal reveals a waterway of startling contrasts. Stretches of tranquil woodland and countryside give way to dramatic mills and historic industry – a reminder of the days when it was the shortest way of carrying goods and people between Lancashire and Yorkshire.

The canal passes by the picturesque town of Marsden, which offers shops, pubs, craft stores and a market. Meanwhile, beautiful Marsden Moor – site of the famous Civil War battlefield – offers walking, angling, cycling and wildlife.

★ Highlights
19th-century viaduct
Spectacular waterfalls
Wildlife

★ Highlights
Standedge Tunnel
Slaithewaite
Marsden

a waterway of startling contrasts

Out into the Countryside

Irwell Sculpture Trail

The Irwell Sculpture Trail follows a well-established 30-mile footpath stretching from Salford Quays through Bury into Rossendale, and up to the Pennines above Bacup.

Following the River Irwell from its source on the South Pennine Moors, to where it becomes the Manchester Ship Canal at Salford Quays, sculptures have been appearing along the trail since 1997. Thanks to an Arts Lottery award in 1996, the project has grown and there are currently around thirty sculptures and environmental art pieces celebrating the area's heritage and landscape. Indeed, the Irwell Sculpture Trail is the largest public art scheme in the United Kingdom, commissioning regional, national and international artists.

The trail passes by, among others, an earthwork sculpture in Peel Park, a specially commissioned 'Lookout' on the lakeside at Clifton Country Park, and a waterwheel sculpture at the entrance to Burrs Country Park. All in all, a fascinating blend of culture, heritage and nature.

Irwell Valley

The Irwell Valley is one of the most picturesque, varied and interesting areas of Lancashire's (and Greater Manchester's) Hill Country – a scenic vale that sweeps down from its source in the South Pennine Moors as far as Salford Quays, on the outskirts of Manchester city centre.

Despite its heavily industrial past, the valley today has been largely reclaimed by the wilds. Along the way are beauty spots such as the Rossendale Valley, whose industrial past lends historic charm to the villages of Bacup, Haslingden, Rawtenstall and Whitworth.

The East Lancashire Steam Railway runs through the Irwell Valley from Heywood, via Bury, to Rawtenstall. The line first opened in 1846 to link the Manchester-Bolton line with Radcliffe. Today, it provides a nostalgic and memorable means of exploring the Irwell Valley. If you prefer to explore the area by foot, follow the unique Irwell Sculpture Trail.

★ Highlights
'Lookout', by Tim Norris
'Untitled', by Ulrich Ruckreim
'Picnic Area', by David Fryers

★ Highlights
East Lancashire Steam Railway
Irwell Sculpture Trail
Rossendale Valley

blend of culture, heritage and nature

reclaimed by the wilds

Out into the Countryside

Jumbles Country Park

With its extensive views of the West Pennine Moors, splendid scenery, woods and reservoirs, Jumbles Country Park is rightly popular with walkers.

The valley and surrounding area have a long and interesting history of industrial activity based on textiles, a factor that has been fundamental in the development of the area for water catchment and storage. The country park was opened in 1971 following the construction of Jumbles Reservoir, and has been popular with visitors and the local community ever since.

Interesting walks are assured all year round. Picnic tables and benches overlook fine views around the Jumbles Reservoir, which is situated at 426 feet above sea level. Meanwhile, a network of footpaths radiate up the valley and across adjacent hills.

Jumbles Information Centre is open throughout the year, with a permanent exhibition on the local and natural history of the area, ideas for other places to visit in the West Pennine Moors and an insight into the water business. Food and refreshment is available at the teahouse.

Leeds-Liverpool Canal

The 200-year-old Leeds-Liverpool Canal is the longest canal in Britain built as a single waterway. It is also one of the least busy, offering a truly tranquil means of exploring the countryside.

Along its 127 miles, the canal passes through 92 locks with the highest lock reaching an altitude of 487 feet. The Rufford Branch links the canal with the Ribble estuary near Preston. The Leigh Branch runs from Wigan to connect with the Bridgewater Canal. At Leeds, the canal joins onto the Aire and Calder Navigation. This last connection means that the canal offers a coast-to-coast route across the North of England.

There are dozens of attractions along the route, while waterway landmarks include the famous Five-Rise flight of locks at Bingley, the impressive Burnley Embankment, and Foulridge Tunnel (through which, according to local belief, a cow once swam).

★ Highlights
Views across the West Pennine Moors
Jumbles Reservoir
Picnic areas

★ Highlights
Bingley Five-Rise
Haigh Hall
Wigan Pier

canal offers a coast-to-coast route

Out into the Countryside

Peak District National Park

The Peak District receives more visitors than any other national park in Europe. Famous for its varied landscape of heather moorland, tranquil dales and the unique geology of millstone grit, the national park is home to a string of idyllic towns and villages from Bakewell and Hartington to Tissington and Buxton.

In the northern portion of the park you can roam on wild open moorland with magnificent views overlooking sites such as the Derwent Dams. Further south, stroll alongside sparkling rivers in wildlife-rich valleys far from the hustle and bustle of the city.

Visit grand houses such as Chatsworth with its farmyard and adventure playground, or the caverns at Castleton, which feature unique Blue John stone, stalactites and stalagmites (and even underground boat rides). There are also stone circles, castles, museums and working mills to explore.

Pennine Bridleway

Not to be confused with the Trans Pennine Trail, the Pennine Bridleway is another important new National Trail – the first purpose-built long-distance bridleway in the UK, providing a fresh challenge for horse riders, mountain bikers and walkers.

Once fully open, it will run from the High Peak Trail in Derbyshire to Byrness in Northumberland – a distance of around 350 miles. Threading through the Pennine hills, the route combines historic packhorse tracks with newly created bridleways. This National Trail is opening in stages: both the 120-mile stretch from Derbyshire to the Mary Towneley Loop and the 10-mile Settle Loop in the Yorkshire Dales are already open.

There are no stiles or steps en route, just wide-open countryside, easy-to-use gates and special road crossing points. The Derbyshire to Mary Towneley Loop is a 5-7 day walk and a 3-5 day cycle/horse ride. The Loop itself is a 3-4 day walk and a 2-3 day cycle/horse ride.

★ Highlights
Chatsworth
The Caverns, Castleton
Derwent Dams

★ Highlights
Rooley Moor
Chee Dale Nature Reserve
Roych Clough

Out into the Countryside

Pennington Flash Country Park

Pennington Flash Country Park is centred on the 'Flash' – a 170-acre lake created through mining subsidence and now nationally renowned for its birdlife. The park also contains an area of woodland and meadows, seven bird hides, a 9-hole golf course, picnic areas, fishing, sailing and an extensive network of footpaths.

Nationally renowned for its birdlife, Pennington Flash is a classic example of natural regeneration. The site lies within the wider 'Heybrook Corridor', which comprises largely agricultural land to the north and west of Pennington Flash, including Amberswood Common, a series of small lakes, ponds and wetlands, and other areas of open water such as Abram Flashes.

Pennington Flash itself constitutes a mosaic of open water, reed beds, scrub and woodland, providing habitats for a wide array of wildlife: 230 species of birds (including local and national rarities), 20 species of butterfly and 16 species of dragonfly have all been recorded in recent years. The site enjoys local protection through designation as a Site of Biological Importance (SBI).

Rivington Pike Route

Situated 1,200 feet above sea level, Rivington Pike and its tower can be seen for miles around. On clear days, views from the tower can reach as far as Blackpool Tower, the Welsh Mountains, the Cumbrian Fells (in the Lake District) and occasionally the Isle of Man (a full 93 miles away).

The hill is reached via the beautiful Terraced Gardens of Rivington, once the magnificent home of Lord William Leverhulme, now owned by North West Water. Burnt down by a suffragette in 1913, the original buildings have lain in ruin ever since. Features include an ornamental Japanese pond, the remains of a swimming pool and a series of arched ornamental bridges.

Self-guided trails weave their way around the surrounding countryside. There's a small exhibition on local and natural history, provided by United Utilities as a resource for the community. The flanks of Rivington Pike are also great cycling territory: the setting was used for mountain biking events during the 2002 Commonwealth Games.

★ Highlights
230 species of birds recorded
Bird hides
Fishing

★ Highlights
Views from the Rivington Pike Tower
Japanese pond
Pigeon Tower

250 species
of birds

104
Out into the Countryside

Rochdale Canal

The Rochdale Canal passes – as you might expect – through the town of Rochdale in Greater Manchester. It is one of three trans-Pennine routes and climbs to quite a height, which means plenty of locks but beautiful views.

The canal runs for 32 miles across the Pennines, from the Bridgewater Canal at Castlefield Basin in Manchester to the Hebble Navigation at Sowerby Bridge in West Yorkshire. In crossing high over the Pennines, the Rochdale Canal serves to join the waterways of the North West with those of the North East. It is a 'broad' canal, allowing boats with a width of 14 feet to pass through its locks. On average there are three locks per mile of canal.

Twenty-five years of restoration work (after much of the route had been obstructed or filled in) saw the canal reopen in 2002.

Rochdale Way

This 50-mile circular route takes walkers through some of the most spectacular countryside of the Borough of Rochdale and the South Pennines, from wooded valleys in the south of the Borough to high open moorland in the north.

The trail provides stunning views across this beautiful pocket of English countryside, and is the perfect way to explore some of the area's most interesting sites. Along the way, you'll pass through pretty river valleys, peaceful woodlands and historic towns and villages filled with grand architecture revealing a proud industrial past.

Most of the route is on public footpaths, but where public bridleways are available, these have been incorporated, so that some sections can be used by horse riders and cyclists. The route in its entirety is a strenuous 50 miles, and most people prefer to split the walk into smaller sections, according to levels of fitness and inclination.

★ Highlights
Sowerby Bridge Basin
Castlefield Urban Heritage Park
Hebden Bridge

★ Highlights
Hollingworth Lake
Healey Dell
Tandle Hill Country Park

three locks per mile of canal

Out into the Countryside

Trans Pennine Trail

Cutting from coast to coast across the spine of England's North Country, the Trans Pennine Trail is an exciting new route for walkers, cyclists and horse riders. It is the first long-distance multi-user trail in the UK, stretching 215 miles between Hornsea in the east and Southport in the west. There are also additional north-south routes between Leeds and Chesterfield and up to York; in total, around 350 miles of trail are available for visitors to explore and enjoy.

The trail is signed and well surfaced, following a mixture of canal towpaths, disused railway paths, cross-country tracks, bridleways, cycle lanes and minor roads. Long sections of the trail are traffic-free and ideal for families with young children. Easy gradients and good surfaces also make much of the route suitable for people using wheelchairs or pushchairs. With so much to discover en route, and with such a wide spectrum of landscapes, journeys along the Trans Pennine Trail can be tailored to everything from day-trips to long expeditions.

Two Brooks Valley

Two Brooks Valley lies deep within Hawkshaw Valley, near Bury. During the 18th and 19th centuries, the valley sustained a community in itself, with a number of mills and farms set alongside several tiny hamlets. The remains of these can still be seen within the valley, while the network of public paths in the area is evidence of the previous industrial activity. These paths, once busy links for horses, carts and workers, now provide the opportunity for a leisurely stroll in the delightful setting of woods, brooks, lodges and fields.

The Valley is home to a great variety of wildlife habitats including grasslands, heath, open water and marsh. Species-rich ancient oak woodland occurs on some slopes, with thriving populations of bluebells, violets and golden saxifrage. Woodlands with these characteristics are ideal habitats for a variety of birds, including the great spotted woodpecker and tawny owl.

Certain parts of the Valley have been officially recognised and protected as Sites of Biological Importance (SBI), including Hawkshaw Brook and Bottoms Wood.

★ Highlights
Windle Edge
Longdendale Valley
St Helens Canal

★ Highlights
Two Brooks Mill
Hawkshaw Brook
Bottoms Wood

350 miles
of trail

Where to Stay

⬛ Hotels

Arora International
★★★★
18-24 Princess Street
Manchester, M1 4LY
(0161) 236 8999
www.arorainternational.com
Newly converted hotel.

Best Western Willow Bank Hotel
★★★
Wilmslow Road,
Manchester, M14 6AF
(0161) 224 0461
www.bestwestern.co.uk
A multi-million pound refurbishment
has enabled this hotel to offer a wide
range of facilities. Ideally located for
the city centre.

Britannia Manchester Hotel
★★★
Portland Street,
Manchester M1 3LA
0845 838 2288
www.britanniahotels.com/
hotel_home.asp?Page=108

Britannia Sachas Hotel
★★★
Tib Street, Piccadilly
Manchester, M4 1SH
(0161) 228 1234
www.britanniahotels.com
Both hotels are both located in the city
centre and boast a range of
restaurants, bars, conference facilities
and well-appointed rooms.

Chesters Hotel and Restaurant
★★★
728 - 730 Chester Road
Old Trafford
Manchester, M32 0RS
(0161) 877 5375
www.chestershotel.co.uk/
home/index.php
An elegant Victorian mansion.

Gardens Hotel
★★★
55 Piccadilly
Manchester, M1 2AP
(0161) 236 5155
www.gardenshotelmanchester.com
A stylish city centre hotel.

Hilton Manchester Deansgate
Awaiting rating
303 Deansgate
Manchester, M3 4LQ
(0161) 870 1600
www.hilton.co.uk/manchester
Taking the wow factor in Manchester
to new heights, this stunning, design-
led, state-of-the-art hotel
accommodates guests in stylish and
contemporary space.

Jurys Inn Manchester
★★★
56 Great Bridgewater Street
Manchester, M1 5LE
(0161) 953 8888
manchesterbudgethotels.jurysinns.com
/jurysinn_manchester
Located in the heart of Manchester,
across the road from G-Mex, MICC
Exhibition Centre and the
Bridgewater Hall.

Malmaison
★★★
Piccadilly, Manchester, M1 1LZ
(0161) 278 1000
www.malmaison.com
Malmaison is an individual hotel for
individual people; known for great
style, friendly staff, great food and
wine and great value.

Novotel Manchester Centre
★★★
21 Dickinson Street,
Manchester, M1 4LX
(0161) 235 2200
www.novotel.com
Just a short walk away from the
commercial hub of the city including
G-MEX and MICC, and the central
entertainment and shopping areas.

Radisson Edwardian Manchester
★★★★★
Free Trade Hall Peter Street
Manchester, M2 5GP
(0161) 835 9929
www.radissonedwardian.com
Luxury 21st-century hotel.

Rossetti Hotel
★★★★
107 Piccadilly, Manchester M1 2DB
(0161) 247 7744
www.aliashotels.com
Situated in the heart of the city, the
Rossetti (soon to be the ABode
Manchester) is a new and exciting
proposition for the city.

Stay Inn Hotel - Manchester
◆◆◆
55 Blackfriars Road
Salford, M3 7DB
(0161) 907 2277
www.stayinn.co.uk
Purpose-built hotel.

The Castlefield Hotel
★★★
Liverpool Road, Castlefield
Manchester, M3 4JR
(0161) 832 7073
www.castlefield-hotel.co.uk
Situated by the water's edge, the
Castlefield Hotel is in an ideal location
or exploring the city centre. Free use
of the health and leisure club.

The Midland Hotel
★★★★
Peter Street
Manchester, M60 2DS
(0161) 236 3333
www.midlandhotelmanchester.co.uk
Set in the heart of Manchester, this
Grade II listed Edwardian building
exudes elegance and style. Luxurious
air-conditioned bedrooms, two bars,
two restaurants and leisure club.

The Princess on Portland
Hotel
★★★
101 Portland Street,
Manchester, M1 6DF
(0161) 236 5122
www.princessonportland.co.uk
Formerly a Victorian cotton
warehouse, the Princess on Portland is
your base in the centre of Manchester.

◆ B&B and Guest Houses

Lyndale Court
★★★
1-2 The Drive, Bury New Road
Salford, M7 3ND
(0161) 792 7270
www.lutherkinghouse.co.uk/
ethical_policy.htm
Bed & breakfast and self catering flats.

Luther King House
★★★
Brighton Grove, Wilmslow Rd
M14 5JP
(0161) 224 6404
A unique location; peaceful and
tranquil.

White Lodge Hotel
◆◆
89 Great Cheetham Street West
Broughton
Salford, M7 2JA
(0161) 792 3047
Small family-run hotel.

◪ Travel Accommodation

Lancashire County Cricket
Club & Old Trafford Lodge
Travel Accommodation
Talbot Road
Old Trafford
Manchester, M16 0PX
(0161) 874 3333
www.oldtraffordlodgehotel.co.uk
Superb 68-bedroom development,
situated at Old Trafford Cricket Ground.
All the rooms are en suite.

Premier Apartments
★★★
64 Shudehill, Manchester M4 4AA
(0161) 236 8963
www.premierapartmentsmanchester.
com
Brand-new Premier Apartments offer
the ideal alternative to a hotel.

Stayingcool
★★★★ / ★★★★★ apartments
Clowes Street, Manchester M3 5NF
Castlefield, Manchester
T: (0161) 832 4060
www.stayingcool.com
Hip hotel meets boutique apartment
suite. Great city centre locations.

YHA Manchester
★★★★
Potato Wharf, Liverpool Road,
Castlefield,
Manchester, M3 4NB
T: (0870) 770 5950
www.yhamanchester.org.uk
'Some call it the best hostel in the
world!' *UK Hostels Guide book.*

Bag the perfect gift at

Manchester
The Gift Shop

Manchester Visitor Information Centre
St Peter Square, Manchester, M60 2LA
+44 (0)871 222 8223

Mon–Sat 10.00am–5.30pm
Sun 10.30am–4.30pm

Manchester
The city break

Discover Manchester's unique flair, style and sheer appetite for life with exciting nightlife, first-class restaurants, superb entertainment, quality accommodation and some of the best shopping in the UK.

Manchester is also home to spectacular events - many of which are free. In the summer months, the city comes alive with live music, festivals and sport. In the winter, the city keeps warm with a festive spirit straight from the continent.

Whether good food at great value, international art and architecture, world class attractions, the best live music or just somewhere to relax, Manchester offers the perfect short break.

www.manchestershortbreaks.com
for the best accommodation deals

0870 609 3013 for a free short breaks guide